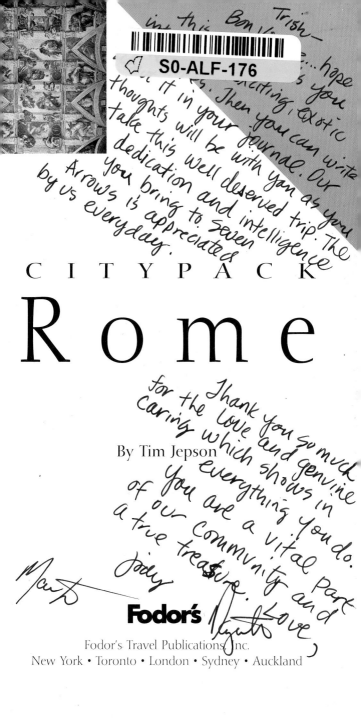

C I T Y P A C K

Rome

By Tim Jepson

Fodor's

Fodor's Travel Publications, Inc.
New York • Toronto • London • Sydney • Auckland

Copyright © 1996 by The Automobile Association
Maps copyright © 1996 by The Automobile Association
Fold-out map:
   © RV Reise- und Verkehrsverlag Munich · Stuttgart
   © Cartography: GeoData

Published in the United States by Fodor's Travel Publications, Inc.
Published in the United Kingdom by AA Publishing

Fodor's is a trademark of Fodor's Travel Publications, Inc.

ISBN 0–679–02961–3
First Edition

Fodor's Citypack Rome

Author: Tim Jepson
Cartography: The Automobile Association
             RV Reise- und Verkehrsverlag
Cover Design: Tigist Getachew, Fabrizio La Rocca

Special Sales

Fodor's Travel Publications are available at special discounts for bulk purchases (100 copies or more) for sales promotions or premiums. Special editions, including personalized covers, excerpts of existing guides, and corporate imprints, can be created in large quantities for special needs. For more information write to Special Marketing, Fodor's Travel Publications, 201 East 50th St., New York NY 10022.

Color separation by Daylight Colour Art Pte Ltd, Singapore
Manufactured by Dai Nippon Printing Co. (Hong Kong) Ltd

10 9 8 7 6 5 4 3 2 1

Page 1: The Sistine Chapel

Page 2 (above): Fontana di Trevi

Page 13 (a): Restoring damaged china

Page 13 (b): Swiss Guard, the Vatican

Page 23: the Colosseum

Page 49 (a): The Dome inside the Pantheon

Page 49 (b): David, Bernini, Galleria Borghese

Page 87: Rome taxis

Contents

About this book

Citypack Rome is divided into six sections to cover the six most important aspects of your visit to Rome.

1. ROME LIFE *(pages 5–12)*
Your personal introduction to Rome by author Tim Jepson
> Facts and figures
> Leading characters
> The big events in Rome's history

2. HOW TO ORGANIZE YOUR TIME *(pages 13–22)*
Make the most of your time in Rome
> Four one-day itineraries
> Two suggested walks
> Two evening strolls
> Four excursions beyond the city
> Calendar of events

3. ROME'S TOP 25 SIGHTS
(pages 23–48)
Your concise guide to sightseeing
> Tim Jepson's own choice, with his personal introduction to each sight
> Description and history
> Highlights of each attraction
> Comprehensive practical information
> Each sight located on the inside cover of the book

4. ROME'S BEST *(pages 49–60)*
What Rome is renowned for
> Roman sites
> Museums and galleries
> Fountains
> Parks and gardens
> Mosaics
> Churches
> Practical details throughout

5. ROME: WHERE TO...
(pages 61–86)
The best places to eat, shop, be entertained and stay
> Eight categories of restaurant
> Eight categories of store
> Five categories of entertainment venue
> Three categories of hotel
> Price levels and booking details

6. ROME TRAVEL FACTS
(pages 87–93)
Essential information for your stay

4

SYMBOLS
Throughout the guide a few straightforward symbols are used to denote the following categories:

✠ map reference on the foldout map accompanying this book (see below)

✉ address

☎ telephone number

◷ opening times

🍽 restaurant or café on premises or nearby

Ⓜ nearest metro station

🚍 nearest bus/trolleybus/tram route

🚆 nearest overground train station

♿ facilities for visitors with disabilities

🔲 admission charge

↔ other places of interest nearby

❓ tours, lectures, or special events

► indicates the page where you will find a fuller description

MAPS
All map references are to the separate foldout map accompanying this book. Where a particular sight appears on both the main map and the large-scale map of downtown Rome (on the reverse of the main map), references to both maps are given. For example, the Palazzo Corsini, on the Via della Lungara, has the following information: ✠ dIV, C6—indicating the grid squares of the large-scale map (dIV) and the main map (C6) in which the Palazzo Corsini will be found. All entries within the Top 25 Sights section are also plotted on the downtown plan located on the inside front and back covers of this book.

PRICES
Where appropriate, an indication of the cost of an establishment is indicated by $ signs: $$$ denotes higher prices, while $ denotes lower charges.

ROME
life

A PERSONAL VIEW

Areas of the city

Rome's ancient heart is the Roman Forum, close to its modern center, Piazza Venezia (though Roman monuments are found all over the city). Via del Corso strikes north to Piazza del Popolo, with the busy shopping streets around Piazza di Spagna

Piazza della Rotonda and (left) the side of the Pantheon

to its east. Corso Vittorio Emanuele II runs west to St. Peter's, bisecting the core of the medieval city (or *centro storico*). Trastevere, a quaint area of restaurants and small streets, lies across the Tiber on the river's west bank. Testaccio, south of the old city, is an increasingly trendy area of bars and clubs. Prati (north of St. Peter's) and the area around Stazione Termini in the east are predominantly 19th-century creations.

Rome, more than most capitals, is a city of extremes. For the first day or so, particularly if you visit during a busy time, the noise, bustle, and traffic can seem almost Third World in their intensity. Arrival at Fiumicino airport, or worse still, the seedy confines of Stazione Termini, can be enough to make you think of turning tail for home. The streets appear places of confusion and wanton crowds, the city a labyrinth of belching cars and groaning inefficiency. Tackle the sights against this backdrop, and in the heat of a summer afternoon, and you will always emerge unenchanted, battered rather than enraptured by what—with the right approach—can be one of the most romantic cities in the world. For if you start slowly, and restrict yourself to a few sights, Rome reveals itself as the city of the Caesars, of languorous sunny days, the city of *la dolce vita*, of art and a galaxy of galleries, of religion, churches and museums, of fountain-splashed piazzas and majestic monuments to its golden age of Empire. To uncover this beguiling, but ever more beleaguered face it is worth ignoring–at least initially–sights such as St. Peter's and the Colosseum (both likely to be besieged by visitors) and start instead with a stroll around the Ghetto or Trastevere, or a quiet cappuccino in Campo de' Fiori or Piazza Navona. Or you might wander into some of the city's greener corners—the Villa Borghese and Pincio Gardens—oases of calm well away from the traffic and streams of people. Better still, start with one of the lesser-known churches, such as Santa Maria del Popolo or San Clemente. Only with this type of quiet beginning, and reassured of Rome's potential for enchantment, can you begin to uncover a city that keeps its magnificent past hidden beneath a brash and initially unsettling present.

Romans Rome itself, however, is not the only thing that can come as a shock, for its citizens can be as startling as their city. In Italy's national mythology Romans are seen as lazy, stubborn, slovenly, and rude, the old joke being that if you follow the famous adage and "do as the Romans do," you would do nothing at all. As ever, there is some truth in the myth. Romans excel in the art of *menefreghismo*—of not giving a damn–an infuriating knack when you want to be served in a bar or seek a little extra space in a bus. Of course there are exceptions, and in their defense Romans have had to develop thick skins to deal with the stresses and strains of living in a city whose facilities barely match its needs (not to mention the flood tide of tourists that further burdens its overstretched resources). This said, a smile and a little stuttered Italian may well bring courtesy instead of gruffness, and after a while the Romans' fabled truculence may even become almost endearing. You might also begin to enjoy the city's almost Fellini-esque cast of characters, from the pot-bellied restaurateurs and dog-walking old women to the fallen aristocrats, grumpy bartenders, and rough-fingered matriarchs of the market stalls.

Vatican City

Vatican City is the world's smallest independent sovereign state (just over 100 acres). Its 200 inhabitants (about 30 of whom are women) are presided over by the pope, Europe's only absolute monarch. Around 800 "foreigners" commute in and out to work, but the general public is only admitted to areas like St. Peter's and the Vatican Museums. The city has its own civil service and judicial systems, shops, banks, currency, stamps, post office, garages—even its own helicopter pad, radio station, and newspaper, *L'Osservatore Romano*. Its official language is still Latin.

One of the matriarchs of the Roman market stalls

ROME IN FIGURES

HISTORY
- Official age of the city (in 2000): 2,753 years
- Number of emperors: 73
- Number of popes: 168
- Water delivered by aqueducts to Rome in the 2nd century AD: 312,000 gallons
- Number of obelisks: 20 (of which Egyptian: 7)
- Number of churches within the city walls: 280

GEOGRAPHY
- Number of historical hills: 7 (Palatine, Celian, Capitoline, Aventine, Quirnal, Esquiline, Viminal)
- Actual number of hills: 20
- Distance from the sea: 17 miles
- Area of the city: 577 square miles

PEOPLE
- Official population: 2,777,882
- Unofficial population: 4,500,000
- Estimated number of tourists annually: 15 million
- Size of average family: 2.7
- Number of people living in illegally built homes: 700,000
- Area covered by illegally built homes: 6,000 acres

RELIGION
- Percentage of Romans with children who have had them baptized: 94
- Percentage of Romans who favor women priests: 40
- Percentage of Romans who do not condemn divorce: 80
- Percentage of Romans who believe in hell: 40
- Percentage of Romans who never go to confession: 60
- Percentage of Romans who sometimes go to mass: 23
- Percentage of Romans who go to both mass and confession weekly: 12
- Percentage of Romans who profess themselves Catholics, but who do not follow the church's "moral teaching": 78
- Percentage of Romans who believe they have been affected by the "evil eye": 37

ROME PEOPLE

Pope John Paul II

THE POPE

Rome's first bishop was St. Peter. Since then his successors have been considered Christ's representatives on earth and held sway over the world's Roman Catholics (today some 850 million). For centuries popes also ruled large areas of Italy (they only relinquished control of Rome in 1870). Papal election—conducted by a conclave of cardinals in the Sistine Chapel—is by one of three methods: acclamation, in which divine intervention causes all present to call one name in unison (not common); by majority vote, with votes cast four times daily until a candidate has a two-thirds majority; and by compromise, on the recommendation of a commission.

VALENTINO

The doyen of Rome's fashion designers has no rivals here. Having risen to prominence in the heady *dolce vita* days of the late 1950s, Valentino quickly established a name for exquisite (and exquisitely expensive) *haute couture*, dressing many stars of stage, screen, and high society. More recently, he has diversified into ready-to-wear and diffusion ranges. To visit his palatial showrooms around Piazza di Spagna, however, is to realize that the master's touch is still appreciated and bought.

Devil's Advocate

The Vatican still has an office for the *Avvocato del Diavolo*—the Devil's Advocate—from which the expression derives. His job is to investigate the lives of prospective saints and those put forward for beatification to discover why they might *not* be acceptable.

The President

Rome is Italy's political capital, and as well as being home to the country's lower and upper chambers (housed in Palazzo Montecitorio—the Chamber of Deputies—and Palazzo Madama—the Senate) it is also home to her head of state, the President (whose offices are in the Palazzo del Quirinale). The post is largely symbolic.

9

A CHRONOLOGY

1200–800 BC	First settlements on the banks of the Tiber
753 BC	Traditional date of the foundation of Rome by Romulus, first of the city's seven kings
616–578 BC	Tarquinius Priscus, Rome's first Etruscan king
509 BC	Etruscans expelled and the Republic founded
390 BC	Rome briefly occupied by the Gauls
264–241 BC	First Punic War between Rome and Carthage
218–201 BC	Second Punic War: Rome threatened by Hannibal, leader of the Carthaginian army
149–146 BC	Third Punic War: Rome defeats Carthage
60 BC	Rome ruled by a triumvirate of Pompey, Crassus, and Julius Caesar
44 BC	Caesar is declared ruler for life but is assassinated by jealous rivals
27 BC–AD 14	Rule of Octavian, Caesar's great-nephew, who as Augustus becomes the first Roman emperor
AD 42	St. Peter the Apostle visits Rome
54–68	Reign of Emperor Nero. Great Fire in 64; "Nero fiddles while Rome burns." Christian persecutions
72	The Colosseum is begun
98–117	Reign of Emperor Trajan. Military campaigns greatly extend the Empire's boundaries
117–38	Reign of Emperor Hadrian
161–180	Reign of Emperor Marcus Aurelius, general and philosopher. Barbarians attack Empire's borders
284–286	Empire divided into East and West
306–337	The Emperor Constantine reunites the Empire and legalizes Christianity. St. Peter's and the first Christian churches are built

Rome is sacked by the Goths after decades of military and economic decline	**410**
Romulus Augustulus is the last Roman emperor	**476**
Charlemagne drives the Lombards from Italy and awards some of the conquered territories to the papacy, the germ of the Papal States. He is crowned Holy Roman Emperor by Pope Leo III	**800**
The Great Schism between rival papal claimants. Papacy to Avignon.	**1378–1417**
The new St. Peter's is built	**1452–1626**
Michelangelo begins the Sistine Chapel ceiling	**1508**
Rome is sacked and looted by German and Spanish troops under Charles V	**1527**
Fontana di Trevi and Spanish Steps begun	**1732–1735**
Napoleon occupies Rome until 1814, when power is restored to the Papal States	**1797**
Uprisings in Rome under Mazzini and Garibaldi force Pope Pius IX to flee. The new "Roman Republic" is ultimately defeated by the French	**1848**
A united Italy is proclaimed but Rome remains under papal control	**1861**
Rome joins a united Italy	**1870**
The Fascists march on Rome and Mussolini becomes Prime Minister. The Fascist regime rules Italy from 1924 to 1943	**1922**
The Lateran Treaty recognizes the Vatican as a separate state	**1929**
Italy enters World War II with the Axis powers	**1940**
The Allies liberate Rome from the Nazis	**1944**
Rome hosts the Olympic Games	**1960**
Karol Wojtyla is elected Pope John Paul II	**1978**
Soccer's World Cup Final held in Rome	**1990**

PEOPLE & EVENTS FROM HISTORY

Capitoline Wolf, suckling Romulus and Remus, Palazzo dei Conservatori (► 37)

ROMULUS AND REMUS

The myth of Rome's birth was recorded by Livy and begins in the old Latin capital *Alba Longa* with the king Numitor, whose throne was stolen by his brother Amulius. To avoid rival claims Amulius forced Numitor's daughter, Rhea, to become a vestal virgin. The god Mars then appeared to Rhea and left her pregnant with Romulus and Remus. The twins, when born, were cast adrift by Amulius, but were guided by the gods to the Velabrum, the old marshes under the Palatine Hill. Here they were suckled by a she-wolf and eventually adopted by a shepherd. In adulthood, fulfilling a prophecy made by Mars, they founded Rome in 753 BC. Both wished to rule, but neither could agree on a name for the new city. Remus favored *Rema*, while Romulus preferred *Roma*. Romulus eventually murdered his brother and built the city's first walls.

The Sack of Rome

One of the single most traumatic events in Rome's long history took place in 1527, when the city was sacked by German and Spanish troops from the imperial army of Charles V. Countless buildings and works of art were destroyed while Pope Clement VII took refuge in the Castel Sant'Angelo. Over 4,000 people died in the siege. The plunder of the city then went on for several weeks.

JULIUS CAESAR

Caesar originally intended to become a priest, joining the army in 81 BC to pay his debts. Rising to the post of *Pontifex Maximus*, Rome's high priest, he joined Pompey and Crassus in 60 BC in ruling Rome as the "First Triumvirate." Over the next ten years he fought military campaigns in Gaul and Germany, and launched two short invasions of Britain. His successes aroused the envy of Pompey, who eventually fled Rome at the news that Caesar had crossed the Rubicon with his returning army. For six months Caesar pursued Pompey across Spain, Greece, and Africa and also spent time with Cleopatra. In 48 BC he was appointed Rome's absolute ruler. He was assassinated in 44 BC on March 15 (the "Ides of March"), murdered by a group of envious conspirators that included Brutus, his adopted son.

ROME
how to organize your time

13

ITINERARIES

Rome is best enjoyed during a short visit by concentrating on a few sights in a single area (having considered opening times) because it is only possible to skim the surface of this great city's cultural and artistic heritage.

ITINERARY ONE	ANCIENT ROME
Breakfast	Latteria del Gallo (➤ 68) or an outdoor café in Campo de' Fiori (➤ 29).
Morning	Stroll through the Ghetto district (➤ 18) to Piazza del Campidoglio Santa Maria in Aracoeli and Capitoline Museums (➤ 37, 38) Roman Forum and the Palatine (➤ 41) Colosseum (➤ 43) Arch of Constantine (➤ 50)
Lunch	Picnic lunch in the Colle Oppio park (➤ 56); snack in Enoteca, Via Cavour 313; or lunch in Da Valentino (➤ 64) or Nerone (➤ 63)
Afternoon	San Pietro in Vincoli (➤ 44) San Clemente (➤ 46) San Giovanni in Laterano (➤ 48) Metro to Termini then Santa Maria Maggiore (➤ 47)
ITINERARY TWO	PANTHEON TO ST. PETER'S
Breakfast	In Piazza della Rotonda or a bar nearby (La Tazza d'Oro, Sant'Eustachio or Camilloni: ➤ 69)
Morning	Santa Maria sopra Minerva (➤ 34) Pantheon (➤ 33) San Luigi dei Francesi (➤ 30) Piazza Navona (➤ 30) Coffee at Bar della Pace (➤ 68) Via dei Coronari or Via del Governo Vecchio Castel Sant'Angelo (➤ 27)
Lunch	Picnic in the Parco Adriano
Afternoon	St. Peter's (➤ 24) Vatican Museums and Sistine Chapel (➤ 25, 26)
Evening	Dinner and stroll in Trastevere (➤ 18)

### THE CORSO TO THE VATICAN	**ITINERARY THREE**
To Via del Corso and the Column of Marcus Aurelius (➤ 51) and then walk to the Fontana di Trevi (➤ 39)	
Bar by the Fontana di Trevi (➤ 39)	**Breakfast**
Walk up Via delle Scuderie and Via Rasella to the Palazzo Barberini (➤ 42) Spanish Steps/Museo Keats-Shelley (➤ 40, 52) Coffee at Caffè Greco or Babington's Tea Rooms (➤ 69) or Casino Valadier (➤ 68) Pincio Gardens (➤ 56) Santa Maria del Popolo (➤ 32)	**Morning**
Picnic in the Pincio Gardens or Villa Borghese (➤ 56, 57) Snack at Casina Valadier (➤ 68) on the Pincio, or Rosati or Canova bars in Piazza del Popolo (➤ 68)	**Lunch**
Ara Pacis Augustae (➤ 31) Walk to Piazza del Risorgimento or take bus 49 from Piazza Cavour Vatican Museums and Sistine Chapel (➤ 25, 26)	**Afternoon**
Stroll and dinner near Piazza di Spagna (➤ 40)	**Evening**
### TOWARDS TRASTEVERE	**ITINERARY FOUR**
Antico Caffè Brasile (➤ 69)	**Breakfast**
Trajan's Markets (➤ 51) Palazzo-Galleria Colonna (➤ 53) Palazzo-Galleria Doria Pamphili (➤ 36) Piazza Venezia: Santa Maria in Aracoeli and Capitoline Museums (➤ 38, 37)	**Morning**
Light lunch in Birreria Fratelli Tempera (➤ 64)	**Lunch**
Walk to Piazza Bocca della Verità via Piazza del Campidoglio and Piazza della Consolazione Santa Maria in Cosmedin (➤ 60) Circus Maximus (➤ 51) Explore the Isola Tiberina Cross to Trastevere and visit Santa Cecilia in Trastevere (➤ 16) Santa Maria in Trastevere (➤ 28) Coffee at Trastè (➤ 68)	**Afternoon**

15

WALKS
FROM PIAZZA VENEZIA TO ST. PETER'S THROUGH THE HISTORIC CITY CENTER AND TRASTEVERE

Temple of Vesta

THE SIGHTS

Santa Maria in Aracoeli (➤ 38)
Capitoline Museums (➤ 37)
Santa Maria in Cosmedin (➤ 60)
(Temple of Vesta: 2nd-century BC
Roman temple)
(Teatro di Marcello: Roman theater
overbuilt with medieval houses)
(San Bartolomeo: 11th century,
over a pagan temple)
(Santa Cecilia in Trastevere: 12th-
century altar canopy, 9th-century
apse mosaic, cloister frescoes)
Santa Maria in Trastevere (➤ 28)
Villa Farnesina (➤ 53)
Palazzo Spada (➤ 53)
Campo de' Fiori (➤ 29)
(Chiesa Nuova or Santa Maria in
Vallicella: frescoes, Oratorio and
clock tower)
Castel Sant'Angelo (➤ 27)
St. Peter's (➤ 24)

INFORMATION

Time 2–4 hours
Distance 3 miles
Start point Piazza Venezia K7
📧 To Piazza Venezia: 44, 46,
56, 60, 61, 64, 65, 70, 75,
81, 87, 90, 170 and others
End point St. Peter's Z9
📧 From St. Peter's: 64 bus to
Largo di Torre Argentina,
Piazza Venezia and Termini
🕐 First see the Capitoline
Museums and the churches
(most close midday). The
Castel Sant'Angelo may be
shut when you arrive.
St. Peter's closes 7PM
(summer), 6PM (winter).
🍴 Trastè (➤ 68)

Start at Piazza Venezia and walk to Piazza del Campidoglio. Exit the piazza briefly in the rear left-hand corner for a view over the Forum. Return to the piazza and follow the alley leading from its rear right-hand corner to Via della Consolazione and Piazza Bocca della Verità. Follow Lungotevere dei Pierleoni north and explore the Isola Tiberina.

Cross Ponte Cestio and follow Via Anicia south to Santa Cecilia in Trastevere. Cut west to Viale Trastevere and Piazza S. Sonnino and follow Via della Lungaretta to Piazza Santa Maria in Trastevere. Leave the piazza to the north and wind through the alleys to reach Vicolo dei Cinque and Piazza Trilussa. If you have time walk west to Via della Lungara to see the Villa Farnesina.

Cross the Ponte Sisto, follow Via dei Pettinari north and then turn left on Via Capo di Ferro to Piazza Farnese and Campo de' Fiori. (Detour south from Piazza Farnese on Via dei Farnesi to look at the elegant Via Giulia and the church of Santa Maria della Orazione e Morte, which is decorated with skulls.) Take Via dei Cappellari west from Campo de' Fiori, turn left on Via del Pellegrino and then right on Via dei Cartari to emerge on Corso Vittorio Emanuele II.

Pick up Via dei Filippini to the left of the Chiesa Nuova. Turn left on Via dei Banchi Nuovi and then right on Via del Banco Santo Spirito. Cross the Ponte Sant'Angelo. Follow Via della Conciliazione to St. Peter's.

WALKS

A CIRCULAR WALK FROM PIAZZA NAVONA THROUGH THE HEART OF THE MEDIEVAL CITY

Begin in Piazza Navona. Leave via the alley in the southeast corner, cross Corso del Rinascimento and follow Via Staderari past Sant'Ivo (within Palazzo di Sapienza) and Sant'Eustachio. Take Via Santa Chiara to Piazza della Minerva and then Via Minerva to Piazza della Rotonda.

Take Via del Seminario east from the Piazza and then turn right on Via Sant'Ignazio and into Piazza Collegio Romano. Cross Via del Corso and wind northeast through Via Santi Apostoli, Via San Marcello, and Via dell'Umiltà to emerge by the Fontana di Trevi.

Follow Via del Lavatore, Via delle Scuderie, and Via Rasella east to the Palazzo Barberini. Walk north to Piazza Barberini and then detour briefly up Via Vittorio Veneto to see Santa Maria della Concezione in the Convento dei Cappuccini. Then west on Via Sistina to the Spanish Steps (Piazza di Spagna). After exploring the Spanish Steps and the chic shopping streets nearby, climb back up to the top of the Steps and take Viale Trinità dei Monte and Viale A. Mickievicz to the Pincio Gardens (and Villa Borghese).

Drop down west to Piazza del Popolo and walk south on Via di Ripetta to the Ara Pacis and the Mausoleum of Augustus. Then from Piazza di Porta di Ripetta follow Via Borghese and Via Divino Amore to Piazza Firenze. Then continue south to Piazza della Rotonda by Piazza in Campo Marzio and Via Maddalena. Take Via Giustiniani west to San Luigi and then follow Via della Scrofa north to Sant'Agostino before returning to Piazza Navona.

Piazza del Popolo

THE SIGHTS

INFORMATION

Time 4–6 hours
Distance 3½ miles
Start point Piazza Navona K7 (circular tour)

🚌 46, 62, 64 to Corso Vittorio Emanuele II or 71, 81, 87, 90,186 to Corso del Rinascimento

🕐 Start early with Palazzo Doria Pamphili and Palazzo Barberini. Churches at the end of the walk are open late afternoon.

🍴 Bar della Pace, Doney, Rosati and Canova (➤ 68); for ice-cream: Tre Scalini and the Gelateria della Palma (➤ 67)

17

EVENING STROLLS

INFORMATION

Ghetto
Start point Via Arenula C6/D6

🚍 Buses 44, 46, 56, 60, 61,
64, 65, 70, 75, 81, 87, 90
to Largo di Torre Argentina;
44, 46, 56, 60, 61, 64, 65,
70, 75, 170, 181 to Via
Arenula and all services to
Piazza Venezia

📷 The empty, echoing streets
of the Ghetto are best seen
late at night.

Trastevere
Start point Piazza San Sonnino C6

🚍 To Trastevere: buses 44, 56,
60, 75, 170, 181 to Piazza
San Sonnino

THE GHETTO

The old Jewish Ghetto occupies the quaint quadrangle of streets and alleys formed by Via delle Botteghe Oscure, Via Arenula, Lungotevere dei Cenci, and Via del Teatro di Marcello. Many descendants of the Jews first forced to move here in 1556 still live and work in the district (there is a synagogue overlooking the Tiber at Lungotevere dei Cenci). Any combination of routes through the area offers intriguing little corners, though the one sight you should be sure not to miss is the charming Fontana delle Tartarughe in Piazza Mattei. This can be seen by walking down Via dei Falegnami from Via Arenula. Thereafter you might wander south on Via Sant'Ambrogio to Via Portico d'Ottavia, where you can see the remains of a 2nd-century BC gateway and colonnade. Striking north from here to Piazza Campitelli and Piazza Margana will also reveal some enchanting nooks and crannies. At night the area, well-lit and almost deserted, should be perfectly safe, though women on their own—as ever—should take special care.

TRASTEVERE

Almost every city has an area like Trastevere (literally "across the Tiber"), a district whose tight-knit streets and intrinsic charm single it out as a focus for eating and nightlife. Trastevere was once the heart of Rome's 19th-century working-class suburbs, and parts of its fringes are still slightly rough and ready (and so worth avoiding in the dead of night). A good way to get to know the area would be to take the Via della Lungaretta to Piazza di Santa Maria in Trastevere from Piazza San Sonnino and then explore some of the smaller streets to the north, such as Vicolo dell Cinque and Via del Moro. At night be sure to take in the floodlit façade of Santa Maria in Trastevere (► 28). During the day, visit the Villa Farnesina (► 53), the Botanical Gardens (► 56), and the market in Piazza San Cosimato (► 73). Time your stroll for the early morning or late afternoon if you want to see the churches in Trastevere, especially Santa Cecilia (► 16).

Fontana delle Tartarughe

ORGANIZED SIGHTSEEING

AMERICAN EXPRESS

American Express runs bus tours around Rome, Tivoli, and farther afield to Pompeii, Naples, and Capri. The Tivoli tour (► 21) (Tue, Thu, Sun 2:30PM) includes Hadrian's Villa and the Villa d'Este. The company also organizes 3–4 hour guided walks of the city with English-speaking guides. These include the "Vatican City" tour (Mon–Sat 9:30AM), which takes in the Vatican Museums (►25), Sistine Chapel (► 26), and St. Peter's (► 24); "Rome of the Caesars" (daily 2:30PM); and "Religious Rome" (Mon, Wed, Fri, Sat 2:30PM), which takes in the Catacombs, Pantheon (► 33), Piazza Navona, and St. Peter's.

➕ D5 ✉ Piazza di Spagna 38 ☎ 67 641 🕐 Mon–Fri 9–5:30, Sat 9–12:30 🚇 Spagna 🚌 119 to Piazza di Spagna

The Tiber and two of its bridges

APPIAN LINE

Many travel agents organize guided tours (several can be found in Piazza della Repubblica). Appian Line, close to Santa Maria Maggiore, is one of the best known. The prices of their tours of the city and destinations farther out are a little cheaper than those of American Express. Booking is unnecessary for local itineraries: simply turn up at the office 15 minutes before your chosen tour departs.

➕ E5 ✉ Piazza Esquilino 6 ☎ 474 6251 🕐 Mon–Fri 9–1, 2–6 🚇 Termini 🚌 4,9,14,16,27 to Piazza Esquilino

GREEN LINE TOURS

Green Line operates trips similar to those organized by American Express and Appian Line at prices about midway between the two.

➕ E5 ✉ Via Farini 5a ☎ 482 7480 🕐 Daily 7AM–9PM 🚇 Termini 🚌 4,9,14,16,27 to Piazza Esquilino

Other reputable firms that run bus tours and guided walks include **CIT**, ✉ Piazza della Repubblica 64 (☎ 47 941), and **Carrani Tours**, ✉ Via V. E. Orlando 95 (☎ 474 2501). CIT, Appian, and Carrani all organize trips on Sunday to the Pope's Sunday blessing at Castel Gandolfo in the Appian Hills. Carrani will also organize papal audiences and (like Appian) a tour of Rome at night with accordianists.

Cheap tours

One of the cheapest and most relaxed tours of Rome can be enjoyed, albeit without commentary, by boarding tram No.19 or 30, both of which meander through some of the most interesting parts of the city. Or take ATAC's official public transportation tour: at 3:30PM daily between April and October (2:30 in winter) the 110 bus makes a 3-hour circuit from Piazza dei Cinquecento (with five stops *en route*). A brief multilingual commentary and a free multilingual brochure are included with tickets, which are available from the ATAC kiosk in Piazza dei Cinquecento from 3PM.

19

EXCURSIONS

Ostia Antica

FRASCATI

Frascati, cradled in the Alban Hills, makes the easiest and most accessible day (or half-day) trip from Rome. Lauded for its white wine, it is also known for its broad views and cooling summer breezes. Small trains ply the branch line to the town, rattling though vineyards and olive groves beyond the city's sprawling suburbs. There is little to do—most pleasure is to be had wandering the streets—but you should see the gardens of the Villa Aldobrandini (above the main Piazza Marconi) and sample a refreshing glass of Frascati in one of the town's many wine cellars.

OSTIA ANTICA

Untrumpeted Ostia Antica is Italy's best-preserved Roman town after Pompeii and Herculaneum, its extensive ruins and lovely rural site as appealing as any in the city itself. Built at the mouth (*ostium*) of the Tiber as ancient Rome's seaport, it became a vast and bustling colony before silt and the Empire's decline together hastened its demise. Among the many excavated buildings are countless *horrea*, or warehouses, and several multi-story apartment blocks known as *insulae*. Other highlights include the Piazzale delle Corporazioni, heart of the old business district; the 4,000-seat amphitheater; and the small Ostiense Museum.

EXCURSIONS

TIVOLI

Tivoli is by far the most popular excursion from Rome (19 miles), thanks to the town's lovely wooded position, the superlative gardens of the Villa d'Este, and the ruins and grounds of Hadrian's vast Roman villa (4 miles southwest). The Este gardens were laid out in 1550 as part of a country retreat for Cardinal Ippolito d'Este, son of Lucrezia Borgia and the Duke of Ferrara. The highlights among the beautifully integrated terraces and many fountains are Bernini's elegant Fontana di Bicchierone and the vast Viale delle Cento Fontane ("Avenue of a Hundred Fountains"). Hadrian's Villa, the largest ever conceived in the Roman world, was built between AD 118 and 135 and covered an area as great as the center of imperial Rome.

Villa d'Este gardens, Tivoli

TARQUINIA

Of great appeal if you have an interest in the Etruscans, Tarquinia (ancient Tarquinii; 70min by train) was one of three major Etruscan cities—the others are present-day Vulci and Cerveteri—and was the cultural, artistic, and probably political capital of the civilization. Founded in the 10th century BC, its population once touched 100,000, declining from the 4th century BC with the rise of Rome. The town's Museo Nazionale houses a fascinating assortment of Etruscan art and artifacts, including the famous winged horses, though it is the number of nearby Etruscan tombs, the Necropoli (many beautifully painted), that draw most visitors (1–3 miles from town).

INFORMATION

Tivoli

- ✉ Villa d'Este, Piazza Trento; Villa Adriana, Via Tiburtina
- ☎ Villa d'Este (0774/22 070); Villa Adriana (0774/530 203)
- 🕐 Villa d'Este: Tue–Sun 9AM–1hr before sunset; Villa Adriana: daily 9AM–90min before sunset.
- 🍴 Refreshments at both Villa d'Este and Villa Adriana. Sibilla, Via della Sibilla 50, Tivoli
- 🚌 COTRAL bus from Via Gaeta or Metro Line B to Rebibbia and COTRAL bus to Tivoli
- 🚆 Train to Tivoli (40min) from Termini and then 30min walk or Villa d'Este (Villa Adriana) local bus No 4
- ♿ Villa d'Este: moderate; Villa Adriana: expensive

Tarquinia

- ✉ Museo Nazionale, Palazzo Vitelleschi
- ☎ Tourist office: 0766/856 384
- 🕐 Museum and Necropoli Tue–Sat 9–2; Sun 9–1
- 🚌 Metro Line A to Lepanto then COTRAL bus from corner of Viale Giulio Cesare and Via Lepanto
- 🚆 Train to Tarquinia from Termini: then shuttle bus to town center
- ♿ Expensive (ticket includes museum and tombs). Contact Museo Nazionale ticket office for tombs.

21

WHAT'S ON

JANUARY	*La Befana* (Jan 6): Epiphany celebrations; fair and market in Piazza Navona
FEBRUARY	*Carnevale* (week before Lent): costume festivities on the streets; parties on Shrove Tuesday
MARCH	*Festa di San Giuseppe* (Mar 19): street stalls in the Trionfale area north of the Vatican
	Festa della Primavera (late Mar–Apr): thousands of azaleas arranged on the Spanish Steps
APRIL	Good Friday (Mar/Apr): Procession of the Cross at 9PM to the Colosseum led by the Pope
	Easter Sunday (Mar/Apr): Pope addresses the crowds at midday in Piazza di San Pietro
	Rome's Birthday (Apr 21): flags and pageantry on Piazza del Campidoglio
MAY	International Horse show (early May): *Concorso Ippico* in Villa Borghese
JUNE	*Feste della Repubblica* (Jun 2): military parade along Via dei Fori Imperiali
	Festa di San Giovanni (Jun 23–24): fair, food, and fireworks around San Giovanni in Laterano
JULY	*Tevere Expo* (last week Jun/Jul): Food and handicrafts fair on the banks of the Tiber between the Cavour and Sant'Angelo bridges
	Festa dei Noiantri (week beginning third Sunday in July): street fairs and processions, Trastevere
	Jazz Festival di Roma (end of Jun/Jul)
AUGUST	*Ferragosto* (Aug 15): Feast of the Assumption; everything closes
SEPTEMBER	Art Fair (Sep): Via Margutta
	Sagra dell'Uva (early Sep): wine and harvest festival in the Basilica di Massenzio
OCTOBER	Antiques Fair (mid-Oct): Via dei Coronari
NOVEMBER	*Festa di Santa Cecilia* (Nov 22): in the catacombs and church of Santa Cecilia in Trastevere
	Ognissanti (Nov 1–2): All Saints' Day
DECEMBER	*Festa della Madonna Immacolata* (Dec 8): Pope and other dignitaries leave flowers at the statue of the Madonna in Piazza di Spagna
	Nativity Scenes (mid-Dec–mid-Jan): crèches (*presepi*) in many Rome churches
	Christmas Eve: Midnight Mass in many churches, especially Santa Maria Maggiore and Santa Maria in Aracoeli
	Christmas Day: papal address and blessing in Piazza San Pietro
	New Year's Eve: firework displays

ROME's
top 25 sights

The sights are numbered from west to east across the city

1

ST. PETER'S

HIGHLIGHTS

- Façade
- Dome
- *Pietà*, Michelangelo
- *Baldacchino*, Bernini
- *St. Peter*, Arnolfo di Cambio
- Tomb of Paul III, Guglielmo della Porta
- Tomb of Urban VIII, Bernini
- Monument to Alexander VII, Bernini
- Monument to the Last Stuarts, Canova
- View from the dome

INFORMATION

- ⊞ bIII, B5
- ✉ Piazza San Pietro, Vatican City
- ☎ 698 4466 or 698 4866
- 🕔 **Basilica** Daily Apr–Sep 7–7; daily Oct–Mar 7–6
  Dome Daily Apr–Sep 8–6; daily Oct–Mar 8–4:45
  Grottoes Daily Apr–Sep 7–6; daily Oct–Mar 7–5
  Treasury Daily Apr–Sep 9–6; daily Oct–Mar 9–5
- 🍴 Shop
- Ⓜ Ottaviano
- 🚌 64 to Piazza San Pietro or 19, 23, 49, 81, 492, 991 to Piazza del Risorgimento
- ♿ Wheelchair access
- 🆓 **Basilica** Free
  Dome and Treasury Moderate
  Grottoes Expensive
- ↔ Vatican Museums, Sistine Chapel, Castel Sant'Angelo (➤ 25, 26, 27)

Although I find the works of art in San Pietro rather disappointing—a Michelangelo sculpture aside—the interior still manages to impress as the spiritual capital of Roman Catholicism with an overwhelming sense of scale and decorative splendor.

History The first St. Peter's was built by Constantine around AD 326, reputedly on the site where St. Peter was buried following his crucifixion in AD 64. Much later, between 1506 and 1626, it was virtually rebuilt to plans by Bramante and later to designs by Antonio da Sangallo, Giacomo della Porta,

Baldacchino and dome

Michelangelo, and Carlo Maderno. Michelangelo was also responsible for much of the dome, while Bernini finished the façade and the interior.

What to see Michelangelo's unforgettable *Pietà* (1499), behind glass following an attack in 1972, is in the first chapel of the right nave. At the end of that nave stands a statue of St. Peter, his right foot caressed by millions since 1857 when Pius IX granted a 50-day indulgence to anyone kissing it after confession. Bernini's high altar canopy, or *baldacchino* (1624–1633), is decorated with bees, symbol of the Barberini family, for Urban VIII, pope at the time of its construction. To its rear are Guglielmo della Porta's Tomb of Paul III (left) and Bernini's influential Tomb of Urban VIII (right). Rome seen from the dome (entrance at the end of the right nave) is *the* highlight of the visit.

VATICAN MUSEUMS

The 1,400 rooms of the Musei Vaticani—the world's largest museum complex—abound in riches: Greek, Roman, and Etruscan sculptures, Renaissance paintings, books, maps and tapestries, and frescoes in the Raphael Rooms and the Sistine Chapel.

Treasures of 12 museums Instead of the two days (and 4 miles of walking) needed to do justice to the Vatican Museums, you can follow one of the color-coded walks, designed to ease your way through the crowds and match the time you have available. Or you might decide on your own priorities, choosing between the collections depending on whether your interest is in Egyptian and Assyrian art (the Museo Gregoriano Egizio), Etruscan artifacts (Museo Gregoriano Etrusco) or in the more esoteric collections of the Museo Missionario Etnologico (anthropology) or the Collezione d'Arte Religiosa Moderna (modern religious art).

Celebrated works of art Whatever your priorities, several sights should not be missed. Most obvious are the Sistine Chapel (► 26), with Michelangelo's recently restored *Last Judgment*, and the four rooms of the Stanze di Raffaello, each of which is decorated with frescoes by Raphael. Further fresco cycles by Pinturicchio and Fra Angelico adorn the Borgia Apartment and Chapel of Nicholas V, and are complemented by an almost unmatched collection of paintings in the Vatican Art Gallery (or Pinacoteca). The best of the Greek and Roman sculpture is the breathtaking Laocoön group in the Cortile Ottagono of the Museo Pio-Clementino. The list of artists whose work is shown in the Gallery of Modern Religious Art is a rollcall of the most famous in the last 100 years, from Gauguin and Picasso to Dali and Henry Moore.

HIGHLIGHTS

- Sistine Chapel (► 26)
- Laocoön
- Apollo del Belvedere (Museo Pio-Clementino)
- *Marte di Todi* (Museo Gregoriano-Etrusco)
- Maps Gallery (Galleria della Carte Geografiche)
- Frescoes by Pinturicchio
- Frescoes by Fra Angelico
- Stanze di Raffaello
- Pinacoteca
- Room of the Animals (Museo Pio-Clementino)

INFORMATION

- ✚ b1, B5
- ✉ Vatican Museums, Viale Vaticano, Città del Vaticano
- ☎ 698 83333
- 🕐 Jul–Sep & Easter, Mon–Fri 8:45–4, Sat 8:45–1; rest of the year Mon–Sat and last Sun of the month 8:45–1. Closed public and religious holidays
- 🍴 Café, restaurant and shop
- Ⓜ Ottaviano
- 🚌 19, 23, 81, 492 to Piazza del Risorgimento, 64 to Piazza San Pietro: connecting bus from Piazza San Pietro to museums
- ♿ Wheelchair accessible routes
- 💰 Very expensive (includes entry to all other Vatican museums)
- ↔ St. Peter's, Sistine Chapel, Castel Sant'Angelo (► 24, 26, 27)

3

SISTINE CHAPEL

HIGHLIGHTS

- Ceiling frescoes, Michelangelo
- Last Judgment, Michelangelo
- Baptism of Christ in the Jordan, Perugino
- Fresco: Temptation of Christ, Botticelli
- Calling of Sts. Peter and Andrew, Ghirlandaio
- The Delivery of the Keys to St. Peter, Perugino
- Fresco: Moses's Journey into Egypt, Pinturicchio
- Moses Kills the Egyptian, Botticelli
- Last Days of Moses, Luca Signorelli

INFORMATION

- bl, B5
- ✉ Vatican Museums, Viale Vaticano, Città del Vaticano
- ☎ 698 3333
- ◉ Jul–Sep and Easter, Mon–Fri 8:45–4, Sat 8:45–1; rest of the year Mon–Sat and last Sun of the month 8:45–1. Closed public and religious holidays
- 🍴 Café, restaurant, and shop
- Ⓜ Ottaviano
- 🚌 19, 23, 81, 492 to Piazza del Risorgimento, 64 to Piazza San Pietro: connecting bus from Piazza San Pietro to museums
- ♿ Wheelchair accessible routes
- 💰 Very expensive (includes entry to all other Vatican museums)

In Michelangelo's frescoes the Sistine Chapel has one of the world's supreme masterpieces. Recently and controversially restored, the paintings of this modest-sized, hall-like chapel at the heart of the Vatican Museums draw a ceaseless stream of pilgrims.

The chapel The Cappella Sistina (Sistine Chapel) was built by Pope Sixtus IV between 1475 and 1480. The Vatican Palace's principal chapel, it is used by the conclave of cardinals assembled to elect a new pope. Decoration of its lower side walls took place between 1481 and 1483, the work, among others, of Perugino, Botticelli, Ghirlandaio, Pinturicchio, and Luca Signorelli. From the chapel entrance their 12 paintings describe *Scenes from the Life of Christ* (on the left wall as you face away from the high altar) and *Scenes from the Life of Moses* (on the right wall).

Michelangelo's frescoes Michelangelo was commissioned by Pope Julius II to paint the ceiling in 1508. The frescoes, comprising over 300 individual figures, were completed in four years, most of which Michelangelo often spent in appalling conditions, lying on his back and in extremes of heat and cold. Their narrative describes in nine scenes the story of Genesis and the history of humanity before the coming of Christ. In the center is the *Creation of Adam*. The fresco behind the high altar, the *Last Judgment*, was begun for Pope Paul III in 1534 and completed in 1541. An extraordinary and unified work of art, crowded with figures and conveying a sense of movement, it shows Michelangelo painting in a more somber mood, the righteous rising to paradise accompanied by angels on Christ's right, the damned drawn irrevocably toward hell on his left.

4

CASTEL SANT'ANGELO

Castel Sant'Angelo, bulwarks rising from the river, has served as army barracks, papal citadel, imperial tomb, and medieval prison. Today its 58-room museum traces the castle's near 2,000-year history and provides a less demanding visit after the Vatican's riches.

Many incarnations The Castel Sant'Angelo was built by the Emperor Hadrian in AD 130 as a mausoleum for himself, his family, and his dynastic successors. It was crowned by a gilded chariot driven by a statue of Hadrian disguised as the sun god Apollo. Emperors were buried in its vaults until about AD 271, when under threat of invasion from Germanic raiders it became a citadel and was incorporated into the city's walls. Its present name arose in 590, after a vision by Gregory the Great, who while leading a procession through Rome to pray for the end of plague saw an angel sheathing a sword, an act thought to symbolize the end of the pestilence.

Castle and museum In 847 Leo IV converted the building into a papal fortress, and in 1277 Nicholas III linked it to the Vatican by a (still visible) passageway, the *passetto*. A prison in the Renaissance, and then a barracks, the castle became a museum in 1933. Exhibits spread over four floors, scattered around a confusing but rewarding array of rooms and corridors. Best of these is the beautiful Sala Paolina decorated with stucco, fresco, and *trompe l'oeil*, though the most memorable sight is the all-round view from the castle's terrace, the setting for the last act of Puccini's *Tosca*.

HIGHLIGHTS

- Spiral funerary ramp
- Staircase of Alexander VI
- Armory
- Hall of Justice
- Fresco: *Justice*, attributed to Domenico Zaga
- Chapel of Leo X: façade by Michelangelo
- Sale di Clemente VII with wall paintings
- Cortile del Pozzo: wellhead
- Prisons (*Prigione storiche*)
- Sala Paolina
- View from Loggia of Paul III

INFORMATION

- dI, C5
- Lungotevere Castello
- 687 5036
- Tue–Sat 9–2; Sun 9–1. Closed public holidays
- Café
- Lepanto
- 23, 64, 87, 280 to Lungotevere Castello or 34, 49, 70, 81, 186, 926, 990 to Piazza Cavour
- Poor
- Expensive
- St. Peter's, Vatican Museums, Sistine Chapel (► 24, 25, 26)

Bernini's Angel, on the Ponte Sant'Angelo

27

5

SANTA MARIA IN TRASTEVERE

HIGHLIGHTS

- Romanesque campanile
- Façade mosaics
- Portico
- Ceiling, designed by Domenichino
- Cosmati marble pavement
- Wall tabernacle by Mino del Reame (central nave)
- Byzantine mosaics, upper apse
- Mosaics on the *Life of the Virgin* (lower apse)
- *Madonna della Clemenza* in Cappella Altemps
- Cappella Avila: baroque chapel

INFORMATION

- ✛ dIV, C6
- ✉ Piazza Santa Maria in Trastevere
- ☎ 581 4802
- ⏰ Daily 7:30–1, 4–7
- 🚌 44, 56, 60, 75, 97, 170, 280, 710, 718, 719, 774, 780 to Viale di Trastevere or 23, 65 to Lungotevere Raffaello Sanzio
- ♿ Wheelchair accessible
- 🎫 Free

One of my most nostalgic memories of nighttime in Rome is of the 12th-century gold mosaics that adorn the façade of Santa Maria in Trastevere, their floodlit glow casting a gentle light over the milling nocturnal crowds in the piazza below.

Early church Among the oldest officially sanctioned places of worship in Rome, Santa Maria in Trastevere was reputedly founded in AD 222, allegedly on the spot where a fountain of olive oil had sprung from the earth on the day of Christ's birth (symbolizing the coming of the grace of God). Much of the present church was built in the 12th century during the reign of Innocent II, a member of a prominent Trastevere family, the Papareschi. Inside, the main colonnade of the nave is composed of reused and ancient Roman columns. The portico, containing fragments of Roman reliefs and inscriptions and medieval remains, was added in 1702 by Carlo Fontana, also responsible for the fountain that graces the adjoining piazza.

Mosaics The façade mosaics probably date from the mid-12th century and depict the Virgin and Child with ten lamp-carrying companions. Long believed to depict the parable of the Wise and Foolish Virgins, their subject-matter is now contested, as several "virgins" appear to be men and only two are carrying unlighted lamps (not the five of the parable). The mosaics of the upper apse inside the church, devoted to the glorification of the Virgin, date from the same period, and represent Byzantine-influenced works by Greek or Greek-trained craftsmen. Those below, depicting scenes from the *Life of the Virgin* (1291), are by the mosaicist and fresco-painter Pietro Cavallini.

CAMPO DE' FIORI

There is nowhere more relaxing in Rome to sit down with a cappuccino and watch the world go by than Campo de' Fiori, a lovely old piazza whose fruit, vegetable, and fish market makes it one of the liveliest and most colorful corners of the old city.

Ancient square Campo de' Fiori—the "field of flowers"—was turned in the Middle Ages from a meadow facing the old Roman Theater of Pompey (55 BC; now Palazzo Pio Righetti) into one of the city's most exclusive residential and business districts. By the 15th century it was surrounded by busy inns and bordellos, some run by the infamous courtesan Vanozza Cattenei, mistress of the Borgia pope, Alexander VI. By 1600 it had also become a place of execution, Giordano Bruno was burned for heresy on the spot marked by the cowled statue.

Present day Crowds of students, foreigners, and tramps mingle with stallholders. shouting their wares. Cafés, bars, and the wonderfully dingy wine bar at No. 15 allow for fascinated observation.

One block south lies Piazza Farnese, dominated by the Palazzo Farnese (begun 1516), a Renaissance masterpiece partly designed by Michelangelo (now the French Embassy). One block west is the Palazzo della Cancelleria (1485), once the papal chancellery. Nearby streets (Via Ginga, Via dei Banllari and the busy Via Cappellari and Via Pellegrino) reward exploration.

Knife-grinder

HIGHLIGHTS

- Street market
- Wine bar Vineria Reggio
- Statue of Giordano Bruno
- Palazzo Farnese, Piazza Farnese
- Palazzo della Cancelleria, Piazza della Cancelleria
- Palazzo Pio Righetti
- Via Giulia
- Santa Maria dell'Orazione e Morte: church door decorated in stone skulls
- Via dei Baullari

INFORMATION

- elll, C6
- Piazza Campo de' Fiori
- No phone
- Market Mon–Sat 7–1:30
- 46, 62, 64 to Corso Vittorio Emanuele II or 44, 56, 60, 65, 75, 170 to Via Arenula
- Cobbled streets and some sidewalk edges around piazza
- Free
- Piazza Navona, Palazzo Spada, Fontana delle Tartarughe (➤ 30, 53, 54)

PIAZZA NAVONA

Piazza di Spagna may be more elegant, Campo de' Fiori more vivid, but the Piazza Navona, with its atmospheric echoes of a 2,000-year history, is a place to amble, watch the world, and stop for a sun-drenched drink at a wayside table.

HIGHLIGHTS

- Fontana dei Quattro Fiumi
- Fontana del Moro (south)
- Fontana del Nettuno (north)
- Sant'Agnese in Agone
- Palazzo Pamphili
- San Luigi dei Francesi (Via Santa Giovanna d'Arco)
- Santa Maria della Pace (Vicolo dell'Arco della Pace 5)
- Santa Maria dell'Anima (Via della Pace)

INFORMATION

- ✚ el, C5
- ✉ Piazza Navona
- ☎ Sant'Agnese (679 4435); San Luigi (683 3818); Santa Maria della Pace (686 1156); Santa Maria dell'Anima (683 3729)
- ◉ Sant'Agnese Mon–Sat 5–6:30PM; Sun 10AM–1PM; San Luigi daily 8–12:30, 3:30–7; Santa Maria della Pace (cloister) Tue–Sat 10–12, 4–6; Sun 9–11; Santa Maria dell'Anima Mon–Sat 7:30AM–7PM, Sun 8–1, 3–7; Palazzo Pamphili: closed
- ⊗ Spagna
- ⊟ 70, 81, 87, 90, 186, 492 to Corso del Rinascimento or 46, 62, 64 to Corso Vittorio Emanuele II
- ♿ Good (Santa Maria della Pace: 2 steps)
- ⊞ Free to piazza and churches
- ⬌ Campo de' Fiori, Castel Sant'Angelo (► 29, 27)

History Piazza Navona owes its unmistakable elliptical shape to a stadium and racetrack built here in AD 86 by the Emperor Domitian. From the Circus Agonalis—the stadium for athletic games—comes the piazza's present name, rendered in medieval Latin as *in agone*, and then in Rome's strangulated dialect as *'n 'agona*. The stadium was used until well into the Middle Ages for festivals and competitions. The square owes its present appearance to the rebuilding (1644) by Pope Innocent X.

Around the piazza Bernini's Fontana dei Quattro Fiumi (1651), the "Fountain of the Four Rivers" (► 54) dominates the center. On the west side rises the baroque Sant'Agnese (1652–7), the façade designed by Borromini. Beside it stands the Palazzo Pamphili, commissioned by Innocent X (a Pamphili) and now the Brazilian Embassy. Further afield, San Luigi dei Francesi is famous for three superlative Caravaggio paintings, and Santa Maria della Pace for a cloister by Bramante and Raphael's frescoes of the four *Sybils*.

Fontana dei Quattro Fiumi

ALTAR OF PEACE

Few ancient bas-reliefs are as beautiful or as striking as those on the marble screens protecting the Altar of Peace, painstakingly but triumphantly reconstructed and restored in its present position from disparate fragments over many years.

Monument to peace Sheltered from Rome's marble-rotting pollution by a glass pavilion, the Ara Pacis Augustae (Altar of Peace) was built between 13 and 9 BC on the orders of the Senate as a memorial to the military victories in Gaul and Spain of the Emperor Augustus, and in celebration of the peace ("*pacis*") he brought to the Empire after years of conquest and civil war. Its panels were buried or dispersed over the centuries, the first fragments being recovered in the 16th century, the last over 300 years later (some were found even as far away as Paris).

Reliefs While the altar at the heart of the monument is comparatively plain, the walls around it are covered with finely carved bas-reliefs. The best occupy the exterior north and south walls, with processional scenes of the altar's consecration, showing the family of Augustus (including his wife, Livia) with 12 *lictors* (with their rods, or *fasces*, symbols of authority) and 4 *flamine* (who light the sacred fires tended in the Forum by the Vestal Virgins). Other scenes include the Lupercalium (the grotto where the she-wolf suckled Romulus and Remus) and Aeneas Sacrificing the Sow (both west panel) and the Earth Goddess Tellus (east panel). The delicate ornamentation below includes floral motifs. Nearby is the Piazza del Popolo, with its range of monuments from the 3,000-year-old Egyptian obelisk to its twin baroque churches and 16th-century gateway.

HIGHLIGHTS

- Emperor Augustus and Family (south wall)
- Emperor Augustus and Family (north wall)
- Aeneas Sacrificing the Sow
- Lupercalium
- Earth Goddess Tellus
- Mausoleum of Augustus (Piazza Augusto Imperatore), to the east
- Piazza del Popolo
- Santa Maria di Montesanto and Santa Maria dei Miracoli (Piazza del Popolo)
- Egyptian obelisk (Piazza del Popolo)
- Porta del Popolo (Piazza del Popolo)

INFORMATION

- ✚ el, D5
- ✉ Via di Ripetta
- ☎ 6710 3569 or 6710 2475
- 🕐 Tue–Sat 9–2; Sun 9–1
- 🚌 81, 90, 926 to Lungotevere in Augusta and Via di Ripetta or 119 to Via di Ripetta
- ♿ Poor
- 🎫 Moderate
- ↔ Santa Maria del Popolo, Pantheon (▶ 32, 33)

31

SANTA MARIA DEL POPOLO

HIGHLIGHTS

- Chigi Chapel
- *Conversion of St. Paul* and *Crucifixion of St. Peter*, Caravaggio
- *Coronation of the Virgin*, Pinturicchio
- Tombs of Ascanio Sforza and of Girolamo Basso della Rovere
- *Nativity*, Pinturicchio
- Fresco: *Life of San Girolamo*, Tiberio d'Assisi
- *Delphic Sybil*, Pinturicchio
- Altar, Andrea Bregno
- Stained glass
- *Assumption of the Virgin*, Annibale Carracci

INFORMATION

- ✠ D4
- ✉ Piazza del Popolo 12
- ☎ 361 0836
- 🕐 Daily 7–12:15, 4–7
- 🍽 Rosati and Canova (➤ 68)
- 🚇 Flaminio
- 🚌 90, 90b, 95, 119, 490, 495, 926 to Piazza del Popolo
- ♿ Few
- 🎫 Free
- ↔ Altar of Peace, Spanish Steps, Villa Borghese, Pincio Gardens (➤ 31, 40, 57)

Santa Maria del Popolo's appeal stems from its intimate size and location, and from a wonderfully varied and rich collection of works of art that ranges from masterpieces by Caravaggio to some of Rome's earliest stained-glass windows.

Renaissance achievement Founded in 1099 on the site of Nero's grave, Santa Maria del Popolo was rebuilt by Pope Sixtus IV in 1472 and extended later by Bramante and Bernini. The right nave's first chapel, the Cappella della Rovere, is decorated with frescoes on the *Life of San Girolamo* (1485–1490) by Tiberio d'Assisi, a pupil of Pinturicchio, whose *Nativity* (*c.* 1490) graces the chapel's main altar. A doorway in the right transept leads to the sacristy, noted for its elaborate marble altar (1473) by Andrea Bregno.

Apse The apse contains two fine stained-glass windows (1509) by the French artist Guillaume de Marcillat. On either side are the greatest of the church's many funerary monuments by Andrea Sansovino, the tombs of the Cardinals Ascanio Sforza (1505, left) and Girolamo Basso della Rovere (1507, right). High on the walls are superb and elegant frescoes (1508–1510) of the Virgin, Evangelists, the Fathers of the Church, and Sybils by Pinturicchio.

Left nave The frescoed first chapel, Cappella Cevasi, also contains three major paintings: the altarpiece of the *Assumption of the Virgin* by Annibale Carracci (above) and Caravaggio's dramatic *Conversion of St. Paul* and the *Crucifixion of St. Peter* (all 1601). The famous Cappella Chigi (1513) was commissioned by the wealthy Sienese banker Agostino Chigi and its architecture, sculpture, and paintings designed as a unit by Raphael.

PANTHEON

No other monument suggests the grandeur of ancient Rome as magnificently as the Pantheon, a temple whose early conversion to a place of Christian worship has left it the most perfect of the city's ancient monuments.

Temple and church Built in its present form by the Emperor Hadrian in AD 119–128, the Pantheon replaced a temple of 27 BC by Marcus Agrippa, son-in-law of Augustus (though Hadrian modestly retained Agrippa's original inscription proclaiming it as his work, which is still picked out in bronze on the façade). Becoming a church in AD 609, it was named Santa Maria ad Martyres (the bones of martyrs were brought here from the Catacombs). It is now a shrine to Italy's "immortals," including the artist Raphael and the first two kings, Vittore Emanuele II and Umberto I.

An engineering marvel Massive and simple externally, the Pantheon (AD 118–125) is still more breathtaking inside, where the scale, harmony, and symmetry—of the dome in particular—is more apparent. The world's largest dome until 1960, it has a diameter of 142 feet (equal to its height from the floor). Weight and stresses were reduced by rows of coffering in the ceiling, and the use of progressively lighter materials from the base to the crown. The central oculus, 29 feet in diameter, floods with light the marble panels of the walls, and the floor paving far below.

HIGHLIGHTS

- Façade inscription
- Interior of the dome
- Cylindrical walls
- The pedimented portico
- Original Roman doors
- The interior pavement
- The open oculus
- Ceiling coffering
- Tomb of Raphael
- Royal tombs

INFORMATION

- ⊞ ell, D5
- ✉ Piazza della Rotonda
- ☎ 6830 0230
- 🕐 Apr–Sep, Mon–Sat 9–6; Oct–Mar, 9–5; Sun 9–1
- 🚇 Spagna
- 🚌 119 to Piazza della Rotonda or 64, 70, 75 to Largo di Torre Argentina
- ♿ Good
- 🎫 Free
- ↔ Santa Maria sopra Minerva, Piazza Navona (➤ 34, 30)

The Pantheon

11

SANTA MARIA SOPRA MINERVA

HIGHLIGHTS

- Egyptian obelisk atop an elephant, Bernini (outside)
- Porch to the Cappella Carafa
- Frescoes: *St. Thomas Aquinas* and *The Assumption*, Filippino Lippi, in the Cappella Carafa
- *Risen Christ*, Michelangelo
- Relics and room of St. Catherine of Siena
- Tombs of Clement VII and Leo X, Antonio da Sangallo
- Tomb-slab of Fra Angelico
- Tomb of Giovanni Alberini by Mino da Fiesole or Agostino di Duccio
- Monument to Maria Raggi
- Tomb of Francesco Tornabuoni, Mino da Fiesole

INFORMATION

- fll, D5
- Piazza della Minerva 42
- 679 280
- Daily 7–12, 4–7
- Spagna
- 44, 46, 56, 60, 61, 64, 65, 70, 75, 81, 87, 90, 170 to Lago di Torre Argentina or 119 to Piazza della Rotonda
- Stepped access to church
- Free
- Pantheon, Palazzo Doria Pamphili (➤ 33, 36)

Almost unique in having preserved (even overpreserved) many Gothic features despite Rome's love for the baroque, behind its plain façade Santa Maria sopra Minerva is a cornucopia of tombs, paintings, and Renaissance sculpture.

Florentine connections Founded in the 8th century over (*sopra*) the ruins of a temple to Minerva, this church was built in 1280 to a design by a pair of Florentine Dominican monks. The connections with Florence continued in the rash of Florentine artists whose work is richly represented in the church: works such as Michelangelo's calm statue of *The Risen Christ* beside the high altar; and the exquisite

Elephant supporting an obelisk

Cappella Carafa, whose finely carved porch is attributed to Giuliano da Maiano. Filippino Lippi painted the celebrated frescoes (1488–1493) of *St. Thomas Aquinas* and the *Assumption*. Among other sculptures are tombs by Mino da Fiesole (of Francesco Tornabuoni, 1480) and perhaps that of Giovanni Alberini with bas-reliefs of *Hercules*, 15th century), Fra Angelico's tomb-slab (1455), the tombs of the Medici popes Clement VII and Leo X (1536) by Antonio da Sangallo the Younger, and Bernini's monument to Maria Raggi (1643). St. Catherine of Siena (one of Italy's patron saints) is buried here; the room in which she died is preserved in the sacristy.

VILLA GIULIA

The Museo Nazionale di Villa Giulia houses the world's greatest collection of Etruscan art and artifacts. Although the exhibits are not always perfectly presented, it remains a revelation for anyone keen to know about the mysterious civilization that preceded ancient Rome.

The Villa Built for the hedonistic Pope Julius III in 1550–1555 as a country house and garden, the Villa Giulia was designed by some of the leading architects of the day, including Michelangelo and the biographer Vasari. Recent restoration has renovated its frescoed loggia and the *Nympheum*, a sunken court in the villa gardens by the Mannerist architect Vignola.

The collection The exhibits range over two floors and 34 rooms, generally divided between finds from Etruscan sites in northern Etruria (Vulci, Veio, Cerveteri, and Tarquinia) and from excavations in the south (Nemi and Praeneste), including artifacts made by the Greeks. Most notable are the Castellani exhibits, decorated vases, cups, and ewers, but with jewelry, dating from the Minoan period, especially, one of the Villa's treasures. Otherwise be selective, picking through the numerous vases, such as the *Tomba del Guerriero* and the *Cratere a Volute*, to see the most striking works of art. These include the *Sarcofago degli Sposi*, a 6th-century BC sarcophagus with figures of a married couple reclining together on a banqueting couch, the engraved marriage coffer known as the *Cista Ficoroni* (4th century BC), the giant terra-cotta figures of *Hercules and Apollo*, the temple sculptures from Falerii Veteres and the valuable relics in gold, silver, bronze, and ivory from the 7th century BC from the Barberini and Bernardini tombs in Praeneste.

HIGHLIGHTS

- *Lamine d'Oro*, Sala di Pyrgi: a gold tablet (left of entrance)
- Vase: *Tomba del Guerriero* (room 4)
- Terracottas: *Hercules and Apollo* (room 7)
- *Sarcofago degli Sposi* (room 9)
- Castellani Collection (rooms 19–22)
- Vase: *Cratere a Volute* (room 26)
- Finds from Falerii Veteres (room 29)
- Tomb relics: Barberini and Bernardini (room 33)
- Marriage coffer: *Cista Ficoroni* (room 33)
- Gardens with *Nympheum* and reconstructed "Temple of Alatri"

INFORMATION

- ✚ D3
- ✉ Piazzale di Villa Giulia 9
- ☎ 322 6571 or 320 1951
- 🕐 Tue–Sat 9–2; Sun 9–1
- 🍽 Café and shop
- Ⓜ Flaminio
- 🚌 52, 926 to Viale Bruno Buozzi or 95, 490, 495 to Viale Washington or 19, 19b, 30b to Piazza Thorwaldsen
- ♿ Good: wheelchair access with assistance
- 💶 Expensive
- ↔ Santa Maria del Popolo, Galleria Borghese (► 32, 45)

13

PALAZZO-GALLERIA DORIA PAMPHILI

HIGHLIGHTS

- *Religion Succored by Spain* (labeled 10) and *Salome* (29), Titian
- *Portrait of Two Venetians* (23), Raphael
- *Maddalena* (40) and *Rest on the Flight into Egypt* (42), Caravaggio
- *Birth* and *Marriage of the Virgin* (174/176), Giovanni di Paolo
- *Nativity* (200), Parmigianino
- *Innocent X*, Velázquez
- *Innocent X*, Bernini
- *Battle of the Bay of Naples* (317), Pieter Brueghel the Elder
- *Salone Verde*
- *Saletta Gialla*

INFORMATION

- ✚ fIII, D6
- ✉ Piazza del Collegio Romano 1a
- ☎ 679 4365
- 🕐 Tue, Fri, Sat, Sun 10–1; closed public holidays
- Ⓜ Barberini
- 🚌 56, 60, 62, 85, 90, 95, 160, 492 to Piazza Venezia
- ♿ Good
- 🎟 **Gallery**: Moderate
  Private apartments: Moderate
- ↔ Pantheon, Capitoline Museums, Santa Maria in Aracoeli, Fontana di Trevi (➤ 33, 37, 38, 39)

Among the largest of Rome's palaces, and still privately owned, the Palazzo Doria Pamphili contains one of the city's finest patrician art collections and offers the chance to admire some of the sumptuously decorated rooms of its private apartments.

Palace Little in the bland exterior of the Palazzo Doria Pamphili prepares you for the splendor of the 100 rooms that lie within. Built over the foundations of a storehouse of classical times, the core of the building dates from 1435, though it has withstood countless alterations and owners. The Doria Pamphili were a dynasty formed by the yoking together of the Doria, a famous Genoa seafaring clan, and the Pamphili, an ancient Roman-based patrician family. Most people come here for the paintings, but for an additional fee you can enjoy a guided tour around some of the private apartments in the 1,000-room palace. The most impressive is the Saletta Gialla, "Yellow Room," decorated with ten Gobelin tapestries made for Louis XV. In the Salone Verde ("Green Room") are three major paintings: *Annunciation* by Filippo Lippi, *Portrait of a Gentleman* by Lorenzo Lotto, and *Andrea Doria*, a famous admiral, by Sebastiano del Piombo.

Paintings The Pamphili's splendid art collection is displayed by ranks of paintings in four broad galleries, numbered not labeled, making a catalogue from the ticket office a worthwhile investment. The finest painting by far is the famous Velázquez portrait of *Innocent X*, a likeness that captured the pope's weak and suspicious nature so adroitly that Innocent is said to have lamented that it was "too true, too true." The nearby bust by Bernini of the same Pope is more flattering.

CAPITOLINE MUSEUMS

With their outstanding but few Greek and Roman sculptures the Palazzo Nuovo and Palazzo dei Conservatori make a far more accessible introduction to the subject than the rambling collections of the Vatican Museums.

Palazzo Nuovo The Capitoline Museums occupy two separate palaces on opposite sides of the piazza. Designed by Michelangelo, the Palazzo Nuovo (on the north side) contains most of the finest pieces, none greater than the magnificent 2nd-century AD bronze equestrian statue of Marcus Aurelius (just off the main courtyard). Moved from outside San Giovanni in Laterano to the piazza here in the Middle Ages, it has recently been restored and placed under cover. Among the sculptures inside are celebrated Roman copies in marble of Greek originals including the *Dying Gaul*, *Wounded Amazon*, *Capitoline Venus*, and the discus thrower, *Discobolus* (▶ 52). In the Sala degli Imperatori is a portrait gallery of busts of Roman emperors.

Palazzo dei Conservatori (detail from the courtyard illustrated above) Former seat of Rome's medieval magistrates, this palazzo contains an art gallery (Pinacoteca Capitolina) on the third floor and a further rich hoard of classical sculpture (second floor). Bronzes in the latter include the 1st-century BC *Spinario*, a boy removing a thorn from his foot, and the 5th-century BC Etruscan *Capitoline Wolf*, the famous she-wolf suckling Romulus and Remus (added later). Paintings in the Pinacotea include *St. John the Baptist* by Caravaggio and works by Velázquez, Titian, Veronese, and Van Dyck.

HIGHLIGHTS

Palazzo Nuovo
- Statue of Marcus Aurelius
- Sculpture: *Capitoline Venus*
- Sculpture: *Dying Gaul*
- Sculpture: *Wounded Amazon*
- Sculpture: *Discobolus*
- Sala degli Imperatori

Palazzo dei Conservatori
- *St. John the Baptist*, Caravaggio
- Bronze: *Capitoline Wolf*
- Bronze: *Spinario*
- Marble figure: *Esquiline Venus*

INFORMATION

- fIV/gIV, D6
- Musei Capitolini (Capitoline Museums), Piazza del Campidoglio 1
- 6710 2071
- Tue 9–1, 5–8; Wed–Fri 9–1; Sat 9–1, 5–8 (winter) 8–11PM (summer)
- 44, 46, 64, 70, 81, 110 and all services to Piazza Venezia
- Poor: stepped ramp to Piazza del Campidoglio
- Expensive (entry to both museums)
- Roman Forum, Santa Maria in Aracoeli (▶ 41, 38)

Constantine, Palazzo dei Conservatori

15

SANTA MARIA IN ARACOELI

HIGHLIGHTS

- Aracoeli staircase
- Wooden ceiling
- Cosmati pavement
- Nave columns
- Tomb of Cardinal d'Albret, Andrea Bregno
- Tomb of Giovanni Crivelli, Donatello
- Frescoes: *Life of St. Bernard of Siena*
- Tomb of Luca Savelli, attributed to Arnolfo de Cambio
- Tomb of Filippo Della Valle, attributed to Andrea Briosco
- Fresco: *St. Antony of Padua*, Benozzo Gozzoli

INFORMATION

- ✚ fIII, D6
- ✉ Piazza d'Aracoeli
- ☎ 679 8155
- 🕐 Daily Jun–Sep 7–12, 4–6:30; daily Oct–May 7–12
- 🚌 44, 46, 56, 60, 64, 65, 70, 75, 90, 90b,170, 492 and all other services to Piazza Venezia
- ♿ Poor: steep steps to main entrance or steps to Piazza del Campidoglio
- 🎟 Free
- ↔ Capitoline Museums, Roman Forum (➤ 37,41)

Detail from the Life of St. Bernard

Perched atop the Capitol Hill, long one of Rome's most sacred spots, Santa Maria in Aracoeli, with its glorious ceiling, fine frescoes and soft chandelier-lit interior, makes a calm retreat from the ferocious traffic and hurrying crowds of Piazza Venezia.

Approach There are 124 steep steps in the staircase, built in 1348 to celebrate either the end of the plague epidemic of 1348 or the Holy Year proclaimed for 1350 (today it is climbed by newly married couples).

Ancient foundation The church was first recorded in AD 574, but even then was old. Emperor Augustus raised an altar here, the Ara Coeli (the Altar of Heaven), with the inscription now on the church's triumphal arch (*Ecce ara primogeniti Dei*— "Behold the altar of the firstborn of God"). Most of the present structure dates from 1260.

Interior Although only one work of art stands out (Pinturicchio's frescoes of the *Life of St. Bernard*, 1486), the overall sense of grandeur is largely achieved by the magnificent gilded

wooden ceiling, built (1572–1575) to celebrate the naval battle of Lepanto (1571), and by the nave's enormous columns, removed from lost ancient Roman buildings. Tombs to inspect include those of Cardinal d'Albret, Giovanni Crivelli, Luca Savelli, and Filippo Della Valle.

16

FONTANA DI TREVI

I can think of no lovelier surprise in Rome than suddenly emerging from the tight warren of streets around the Fontana di Trevi to be confronted with the city's most famous fountain—a sight "silvery to the eye and ear" in the words of Charles Dickens.

Virgin discovery In its earliest guise the Fontana di Trevi marked the end of the Aqua Virgo, or Acqua Vergine, an aqueduct built by Agrippa in 19 BC (supposedly filled with Rome's sweetest waters). The spring feeding it was reputedly discovered by a virgin, hence its name (she is said to have shown her discovery to some Roman soldiers, a scene—along with Agrippa's approval of the aqueduct's plans—which is described in bas-reliefs on the fountain's second tier). Its liveliness and charm is achieved by the pose of *Oceanus*, the central figure, and the two giant tritons and their horses symbolizing a calm and a stormy sea, drawing his chariot. Other statues represent Abundance and Health and, above, the Four Seasons, which each carry gifts.

Fountains A new fountain was built in 1453 on the orders of Pope Niccolò V, who paid for it by levying a tax on wine (Romans sneered that he "took our wine to give us water"). Its name came from the three roads (*tre vie*) that converged on the piazza. The present fountain was commissioned by Pope Clement XII in 1732 and finished 30 years later: its design—inspired by the Arch of Constantine—is attributed to Nicola Salvi, with possible contributions from Bernini (though the most audacious touch—combining a fountain with a palace-like façade—was probably the work of Pietro da Cortona). Visitors wishing to return to Rome throw a coin (preferably over the shoulder) into the fountain. The money goes to the Italian Red Cross.

HIGHLIGHTS

- *Oceanus* (Neptune)
- *Allegory of Health* (right of *Oceanus*)
- *Virgin Indicating a Spring to Soldiers*
- *Allegory of Abundance* (left of *Oceanus*)
- *Agrippa Approving the Design of the Aqueduct*
- *Triton with Horse* (on the right symbolizing the ocean in repose)
- *Triton with Horse* (on the left symbolizing a tempestuous sea)
- Façade of Santi. Vincenzo e Anastasio
- Baroque interior of Santa Maria in Trivio

INFORMATION

- ⊞ fll/gll, D5
- ✉ Piazza Fontana di Trevi
- 🕐 Always open
- Ⓢ Spagna or Barberini
- 🚌 52, 53, 56, 58, 60, 61, 62, and other routes to Via del Corso and Via del Tritone
- ♿ Access via cobbled street
- 🎫 Free
- ↔ Spanish Steps, Palazzo Doria Pamphili (► 40, 36)

17

SPANISH STEPS

HIGHLIGHTS

- Spanish Steps
- Museo Keats–Shelley (➤ 52)
- Trinità dei Monte
- Fontana della Barcaccia (➤ 54)
- Babington's Tea Rooms (➤ 69)
- Caffè Greco (➤ 69)
- Villa Medici gardens
- Pincio Gardens (➤ 56)
- Roffi Isabelli: wine bar and shop, Via della Croce 76a

INFORMATION

- fl/gl, D5
- Piazza di Spagna
- Museo Keats–Shelley (678 4235); Babington's Tea Rooms (678 6027); Caffè Greco (679 1700); Villa Medici (679 8381)
- **Spanish Steps**: always open
- **Museo Keats–Shelley**: Mon–Fri 9–1, 3–6
- **Trinità dei Monte**: daily 10–12:30, 4–6
- **Villa Medici**: Occasionally open for exhibitions
- **gardens:** apply to the French Academy
- Caffè Greco, Babington's Tea Rooms
- Spagna
- 119 to Piazza di Spagna
- None for the Spanish Steps
- Free except to Museo Keats–Shelley (moderate)
- Palazzo Barberini, Santa Maria del Popolo (➤ 42, 32)

Neither old nor particularly striking, the Spanish Steps are nonetheless one of Rome's most famous sights, thanks largely to their popularity as a meeting point, to their views, and to their position at the heart of the city's most exclusive shopping district.

Spanish Steps Despite their name, the Spanish Steps were commissioned by a Frenchman, Gueffier (the French ambassador), who in 1723 sought to link Piazza di Spagna with the French-owned church of Trinità dei Monte on the hill above. A century earlier the piazza had housed the headquarters of the Spanish ambassador to the Holy See, hence the name of both the Steps and the square.

Around the Steps At the base of the Steps sits the Fontana della Barcaccia, commissioned in 1627 by Urban VIII and designed either by Gian Lorenzo Bernini or perhaps his less famous father, Pietro. The design represents a half-sunken boat (➤ 54). To the right of the Steps stands the Museo Keats–Shelley (➤ 52), a fascinating collection of literary memorabilia and a working library housed in the lodgings where the poet John Keats died in 1821. To the right is the famed Babington's Tea Rooms (➤ 69) and to the south the Via Condotti, Rome's most exclusive shopping street. At the top of the Steps turn to enjoy the views past the Palazzo Barberini and towards the Quivinal Hill, walk into the simple Trinità dei Monte, with its outside double staircase by Domenico Fontana, and visit the beautiful 16th-century gardens of the 16th-century Villa Medici (open one or two days each week), the seat of the French Academy, where students can study painting, sculpture, architecture, engraving, and music.

ROMAN FORUM

The Roman Forum was the civic and political heart of the Roman Empire. The mosaic of ruins can be difficult to decipher, but the site is one of the most evocative in the city, the standing stones and fragments bringing echoes of a once all-powerful state.

History The Forum (Foro Romano) started life as a marsh between the Palatine and Capitoline hills, taking its name from a word meaning "outside the walls." Later it became a rubbish dump, and (after drainage) a marketplace, and religious shrine. In time it acquired all the structures of Rome's burgeoning civic, social and political life. Consuls, emperors, and senators embellished it with magnificent temples, courts, and basilicas.

Forum and Palatine A 1,000-year history, and two millennia of plunder and decay have left a mishmish of odd pillars and jumbled stones, which can make vivid sense, given a plan and imagination. Nonetheless, this strange, empty space is romantic , especially on the once palace-covered Palatine Hill to the south. Today orange trees, oleander and cypress line the paths; grasses and wildflowers flourish among the ancient remains. Worth a visit are the Temple of Antonius and Faustina, the Colonna di Foca, the Curia, the restored Arch of Septimius Severus, the Portico of the Dei Consentes, the Temple of Saturn, Santa Maria Antiqua, the oldest church in the Forum, the House of the Vestal Virgins, who tended the sacred fire, the aisle of the Basilica of the Emperor Maxentius, and the Arch of Titus.

HIGHLIGHTS

- Tempio di Antonino e Faustina (AD 141, a church in medieval times)
- Colonna di Foca (AD 608)
- Curia (Senate House, 80 BC)
- Arco di Settimio Severo (AD 203)
- 12 columns from the Portico of the Dei Consentes (AD 367)
- 8 columns from the Tempio di Saturno (42 BC, AD 284)
- House of the Vestal Virgins

INFORMATION

- ✚ gIV, D6/E6
- ✉ Entrances from Via di San Gregorio and at Largo Romolo e Remo on Via dei Fori Imperiali
- ☎ 699 0110
- 🕐 Mon, Wed–Sat 9 till 2 hours before sunset; Tue & Sun 9–2
- 🚇 Colosseo
- 🚌 11, 27, 81, 85, 87, 186 to Via dei Fori Imperiali
- ♿ Access only from Largo Romolo e Remo
- 💶 Expensive (includes entry to the Palatine and Farnese Gardens, ➤ 56)
- ↔ Colosseum, Capitoline Museums, Arch of Constantine, San Clemente (➤ 43, 37, 50, 46)

Pillar and capital from the Forum

19

PALAZZO BARBERINI

The magnificent Palazzo Barberini—designed by Bernini, Borromini, and Carlo Maderno—also houses a stupendous ceiling fresco and one of Rome's finest art collections, the Galleria Nazionale d'Arte Antica (the earlier works of the Galleria Nazionale).

HIGHLIGHTS

- Central windows and Scala Elicoidale
- *Madonna and Child* and *Annunciation*, Filippo Lippi (room II)
- *Holy Family* and *Madonna and Saints*, Andrea del Sarto (room V)
- *Madonna and Child*, Beccafumi (room V)
- *La Fornarina*, Raphael (room XIV)
- *Adoration of the Shepherds* and *Baptism of Christ*, El Greco (room IX)
- *Judith and Holofernes* and *Narciso*, Caravaggio (room XIV)
- *Beatrice Cenci*, attributed to Guido Reni (room XVIII)
- *Henry VIII*, attributed to Holbein (room XIX)
- *The Triumph of Divine Providence* (Gran Salone)

INFORMATION

- hI, E5
- Via delle Quattro Fontane 13
- 481 4591 or 482 4184
- Tue–Sat 9–2, Sun and public holidays 9–1
- Barberini
- 52, 53, 56, 58, 58b, 60, 95, 119, 492 to Via del Tritone or 57, 64, 65, 70, 71, 75, 170 to Via Nazionale
- Few
- Moderate
- Spanish Steps, Santa Maria Maggiore (➤ 40, 47)

The Palace The Palazzo Barberini (Galleria Nazionale d'Arte Antica) was commissioned by Maffei Barberini for his family when he became Pope Urban VIII in 1623. The epitome of Rome's high baroque style, it is a maze of suites, apartments, and staircases, many still swathed in their sumptuous original decoration. Overshadowing all is the Gran Salone, dominated by Pietro da Cortona's rich ceiling frescoes, glorifying Urban as an agent of Divine Providence. The central windows and oval spiral staircase (Scala Elicoidale) are Borromini's creation.

The collection *Antica* here means old rather than ancient, and embraces the earlier part of the nation's art collection. Probably its most popular picture is Raphael's *La Fornarina* (also attributed

to Giulio Romano), reputedly a portrait of one of the artist's mistresses, identified later as the daughter of a baker (*fornaio* means baker). It was executed in the year of the painter's death, a demise brought on, it is said, by his mistress's unrelenting passion.

Raphael's La Fornarina

Eminent Italian works from Filippo Lippi, Andrea del Sarto, Caravaggio, and Guido Reni are contrasted with foreign artists.

COLOSSEUM

The Pantheon may be better preserved, the Forum more historically important, but for me no other monument in Rome rivals the majesty of the Colosseum, the world's largest surviving structure from Roman antiquity.

History The Colosseum (Colosseo) was begun by the Emperor Vespasian in AD 72 and inaugurated by his son, Titus, in AD 80 with a gala that saw 5,000 animals slaughtered in a day (and 100 days of continuous games thereafter). Finishing touches to the 55,000-seat stadium were added by Domitian (AD 81–96). Its walls are made of brick and volcanic tufa faced with travertine marble blocks, which were bound together by metal clamps (removed AD 664), and three types of columns support the arcades. Its long decline began in the Middle Ages, with the pillaging of stone for churches and palaces. The desecration ended in 1744, when the structure was consecrated in memory of the Christians supposedly martyred there. Clearing of the site and excavations began late in the 19th century and restoration was carried out in the 20th.

Games Christian martyrdoms, however, were rare events, unlike the gladitorial games, which continued for some 500 years. Criminals, slaves and gladiators, and wild animals kept underground, fought usually to the death. Women and dwarfs also wrestled, and mock sea battles were waged, the arena being flooded in minutes via underground drains. Spectators could exercise the power of life and death, waving handkerchiefs to signify mercy or by the famous down-turned thumb. Survivors often had their throats cut anyway, and even the dead were poked with red-hot irons to make sure they had actually expired.

HIGHLIGHTS

- Circumference walls
- Arches: 80 lower arches for the easy admission of crowds
- Doric columns: lowest arcade
- Ionic columns: central arcade
- Corinthian columns: upper arcade
- Underground rooms for animals
- The "holes" used by the binding metal clamps
- *Vomitoria*: interior exits and entrances
- Views from the upper levels
- Arch of Constantine nearby (➤ 50)

INFORMATION

- ✚ hIV, E6
- ✉ Piazza del Colosseo, Via dei Fori Imperiali
- ☎ 700 4261
- 🕐 Mon, Tue, Thu–Sat 9–2 hours before sunset; Wed, Sun 9–1
- 🚇 Colosseo
- 🚌 11, 13, 15, 27, 30b, 81, 85, 87, 118, 186, 673 to Piazza del Colosseo
- ♿ Poor to the interior: limited access from Via Celio Vibenna entrance
- 🎟 **Ground floor** Free **Upper levels** Moderate
- ↔ Roman Forum, San Clemente, Capitoline Museums, San Pietro in Vincoli, Arch of Constantine (➤ 41, 46, 37, 44, 50)

21

SAN PIETRO IN VINCOLI

HIGHLIGHTS

- Moses, Michelangelo
- Profile self-portrait in the upper part of Moses' beard
- Chains of St. Peter
- Carved paleochristian sarcophgus (crypt)
- Mosaic: *St. Sebastian*
- Tomb of Niccolò da Cusa
- *Santa Margherita* by Guercino
- Tomb of Antonio and Piero Pollaiuolo
- Torre dei Margani (Piazza San Pietro in Vincoli), once believed to have been owned by the Borgias

INFORMATION

- ✚ hIII, E6
- ✉ Piazza di San Pietro in Vincoli 4a
- ☎ 488 2865
- 🕐 Mon–Sat 7–12:30, 3:30–7 (Oct–Mar 6PM); Sun 8:45–11:30AM
- 🚇 Colosseo or Cavour
- 🚌 11, 27, 81 to Via Cavour or 11, 27, 81, 85, 87, 186 to Piazza del Colosseo
- ♿ Good
- 🆓 Free
- ↔ Colosseum, Roman Forum (➤ 43, 41)

San Pietro in Vincoli, hidden in a narrow back street, is a thoroughly appealing church. I have often dropped in to admire Michelangelo's statue of Moses, one of the most powerful of all the artist's monumental sculptures.

Chains San Pietro in Vincoli takes its name from the chains (*vincoli*) proudly clasped in the coffer with bronze doors under the high altar. According to tradition they are the chains used to bind St. Peter while he was held captive in the Mamertine prison (remnants of which are preserved under the church of San Giuseppe near the Forum). Part of the chains found their way to Constantinople, while the rest were housed in San Pietro by Pope Leo I (who had the church specially reconstructed from a 4th-century building for the purpose). When the two parts were eventually reunited, they are said to have miraculously fused together. The church has often been transformed and restored. The 20 columns of its interior arcade came originally from a Roman temple.

Works of art Michelangelo's majestic sculpture, of a patriarchal Moses receiving the Tablets of Stone, was originally designed as part of a 42-figure ensemble for the tomb of Julius II. Michelangelo spent years scouring the Carrara mountains for suitable pieces of stone, but the project never came close to completion, and he was to describe the work as "this tragedy of a tomb"; much of his time (reluctantly) was spent instead on the Sistine Chapel. Also make sure you see the Byzantine mosaic (*c.* 680) of *St. Sebastian*, the monument to the Pollaiuolo brothers (*c.* 1498) by Luigi Capponi and the tomb of Cardinal da Cusa (1464), attributed to Andrea Bregno.

GALLERIA BORGHESE

Normally only the collection of the Vatican Museums would surpass the sculptures and paintings of the Galleria Borghese. Since subsidence in 1985, however, only the sculptures now reside here, the paintings being housed at San Michele a Ripa.

Seductress The Villa Borghese was designed in 1613 as a summer retreat for Cardinal Scipione Borghese, nephew of Pope Paul V, who accumulated most of the collection (acquired by the state in 1902). Scipione was an enthusiastic patron of Bernini, whose works dominate the gallery. The museum's first masterpiece, however, is Antonio Canova's *Paolina Borghese* (above), Napoleon's sister, and wife of Camillo Borghese. Depicted bare-breasted, with a come-hither hauteur,
Paolina was just as slyly seductive in life. She excited gossip through her jewels, her clothes, her lovers, and the servants she used as footstools.

Bernini His *David* (1623–4) is said to be a self-portrait (sculpted while Scipione held the mirror). *Apollo and Daphne* (1622–5) in the

Temple of Aesculapius, Villa Borghese

next room, is considered his masterpiece. Other Bernini works include the *Rape of Proserpine* (1622) and *Truth Unveiled by Time* (1652).

The paintings Foremost among this treasure-trove are works by Raphael (*The Deposition of Christ*), Titian (*Sacred and Profane Love*), Caravaggio (*Boy with a Fruit Basket* and *Madonna dei Palafrenieri*), and Correggio (*Danae*).

HIGHLIGHTS

Galleria Borghese
- *Paolina Borghese*, Canova
- *David*, Bernini
- *Apollo and Daphne*, Bernini

Quadreria della Galleria Borghese al San Michele a Ripa
- *Madonna dei Palafrenieri*, Caravaggio
- *Sacred and Profane Love*, Titian
- *Deposition of Christ*, Raphael

INFORMATION

Galleria Borghese
- ✚ E4
- ✉ Piazzale Scipione Borghese 5
- ☎ 854 8577
- 🕐 Tue–Sat 9–2; Sun 9–1. Closed public holidays
- Ⓜ Spagna or Flaminio
- 🚌 52, 53, 910 to Via Pinciana or 3, 4, 56, 57, 319 to Via Po or 19, 30b to Via delle Belle Arti
- ♿ Steps to front entrance
- 💲 Moderate
- ♿ Villa Giulia (➤ 35)

San Michele a Ripa in Trastevere
- ✚ C7
- ✉ Via di San Michele in Trastevere
- ☎ 581 6732
- 🕐 Tue–Sat 9–2; Sun 9–1
- 🚌 13, 23 to Viale di Trastevere
- 💲 Moderate

45

SAN CLEMENTE

For me, no site in Rome suggests as vividly the layers of history that underpin the city as San Clemente, a beautiful medieval ensemble built over a superbly preserved 4th-century church and the remains of a 3rd-century Mithraic temple.

Upper church The present San Clemente—named after Rome's fourth pope—was built between 1108 and 1184 following the sack of an earlier church here by the Normans in 1084. Almost untouched since, its medieval interior is dominated by the earlier 12th-century marble panels of the choir screen and pulpits and the glittering 12th-century apse mosaic, *Trionfo della Croce*. Equally captivating are frescoes (1428–31) on the *Life of St. Catherine* by Masolino da Panicale.

Mithraic temple

Underground sanctuaries Steps descend to the lower church, sacked by the Normans, with traces of its 8th- to 11th-century frescoes of San Clemente and the legends of Sts. Alessio and Sisinnio. More steps lead deeper into the twilight world of the best-preserved of the 12 Mithraic temples uncovered in Rome. (Mithraism was a popular, male-only cult, eclipsed by Christianity.) Here are an altar with a bas-relief of Mithras, and the Triclinium, used for banquets and rites. Excavations are revealing parts of the temple, and the 1,900-year-old remains of other buildings, streets, and an (audible) underground stream that perhaps formed part of ancient Rome's drainage system.

SANTA MARIA MAGGIORE

Santa Maria Maggiore is Rome's finest early Christian basilica, with a magnificent interior that celebrates its long history; it is the only church in the city where Mass has been celebrated every single day since the 5th century.

History According to myth, the Virgin appeared to Pope Liberius on August 5, AD 352, telling him to build a church exactly where snow would fall the next day. Although it was summer, the snow fell, marking the outlines of a basilica on the Esquiline Hill. Legend aside, the church probably dates from AD 430, though the campanile (at 246 feet the tallest in Rome) was added in 1377, and the interior and exterior were altered in the 13th and 18th centuries. The coffered ceiling, attributed to Giuliano da Sangallo, was reputedly gilded with the first gold to arrive from the New World, a gift from Spain to Alexander VI (note his Borgia bull emblems).

Interior Beyond the splendor of its general decoration, the main treasures are mosaics: 36 panels from then 5th-century in the architraves of the nave on the *Lives of Moses, Abraham, Isaac, and Jacob* (framed below by some 40 ancient columns); on the Triumphal Arch of the *Annunciation* and *Infancy of Christ*; Jacopo Torriti's 13th-century apse mosaics, including the *Coronation of the Virgin* (1295), the pinnacle of Rome's medieval mosaic tradition; and those in the entrance loggia by Filippo Rusuti. Other highlights include the Cappella Sistina (tomb of Sixtus V, by Domenico Fontana, 1588) and Cappella Paolina, built by rival popes, and Giovanni di Cosima's tomb of Cardinal Rodriguez (1299). The high altar reputedly contains relics of Christ's crib, the object of devotion of countless pilgrims.

HIGHLIGHTS

- Mosaics: upper tier of entrance loggia
- Coffered ceiling
- Mosaic cycle: 36 Old Testament scenes
- Mosaics: Triumphal Arch
- Apse mosaic: *Coronation of the Virgin*, Jacopo Torriti
- Four reliefs from a papal altar, Mino del Reame
- Fresco fragments: *Prophets*, attributed to Cimabue, Pietro Cavallini, or Giotto (apse)
- Cappella Sistina
- Cappella Paolina
- Tomb of Cardinal Rodriguez, Giovanni di Cosima

INFORMATION

- 🔢 E6
- ✉️ Piazza di Santa Maria Maggiore and Piazza dell'Esquilino
- ☎️ 483 195
- 🕐 Daily Apr–Sep 7AM–8PM; daily Oct–March 7AM–7PM
- 🚇 Termini or Cavour
- 🚌 16, 27, 70, 71, 93, 93b to Piazza di Santa Maria Maggiore
- ♿ Poor: access is easiest from Piazza di Santa Maria Maggiore
- 🎫 Free
- ↔️ San Pietro in Vincoli, Palazzo Barberini (➤ 44, 42)

SAN GIOVANNI IN LATERANO

HIGHLIGHTS

- Central portal: bronze doors
- Fresco: *Boniface VIII*, attributed to Giotto
- Cappella Corsini
- Frescoed tabernacle
- High altar reliquary
- Apse mosaic, Jacopo Torriti
- Cloister: columns and inlaid marble mosaics
- Papal altar: only the Pope can celebrate Mass here
- Scala Santa
- Baptistery

INFORMATION

- ✚ F7
- ✉ Piazza di San Giovanni in Laterano
- ☎ 698 86452
- ◑ **Church & Cloister**
  Apr–Sep, daily 7AM–7PM;
  Oct–Mar, daily 7AM–6PM
- **Scala Santa** Summer daily 6–midday, 2:30–6:30; winter daily
- **Baptistery** Daily 9–1, 4–6
- **Museum** Mon–Fri 9–1, 3–5
- 🚇 San Giovanni
- 🚌 4, 15, 16, 85, 87, 93, 93b, tram 13, 30b to Piazza di San Giovanni in Laterano
- ♿ Poor: steps to church
- 🎟 **Church, Scala Santa, Baptistery** Free
  Museum and Cloister Inexpensive
- ↔ San Clemente, San Pietro in Vincoli (➤ 46, 44)

San Giovanni's façade can be seen from afar, its statues rising over the rooftops—a deliberate echo of St. Peter's—reminding us that this is the cathedral church of Rome and the Pope's titular see in his role as Bishop of Rome.

History A 4th-century palace here provided a meeting place for Pope Miltiades and Constantine (the first Christian emperor) and then became a focus for Christianity. Barbarians, earthquakes, and fires destroyed the earliest churches on the site; the façade (modeled on St. Peter's) dates from 1735, Borromini's interior from 1646. It was the papal residence in Rome until the 14th century (when the popes moved to the Vatican), though pontiffs were crowned here until the 19th century.

Nave with statues of the Apostles

Interior Bronze doors from the Forum's Curia usher you into the cavernous interior, its chill whites and grays redeemed by a fabulously ornate ceiling. The cloister provides the main attraction, although al fresco, of *Boniface VIII*, attributed to Giotto, and an apse mosaic is by Jacopo Torriti. A high altar reliquary is supposed to contain the heads of Sts. Peter and Paul and a frescoed tabernacle is attributed to Arnolfo di Cambio and Fiorenzo de Lorenzo. Outside are the Scala Santa, reputedly the steps ascended by Christ at his trial in Jerusalem (the faithful climb up on their knees). The octagonal Baptistery dates back to the time of Constantine and was the model for many subsequent baptisteries.

ROME's
best

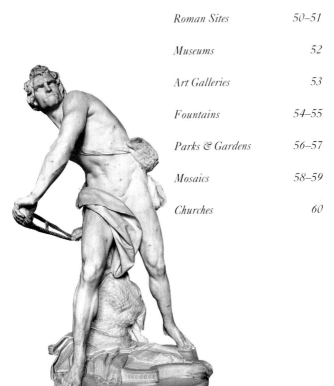

49

ROMAN SITES

Triumphal arches

Two of Rome's greatest contributions to architecture were the basilica and the triumphal arch, the latter raised by the Roman Senate on behalf of a grateful populace to celebrate the achievements of victorious generals and emperors. Returning armies and their leaders would pass through the arches, bearing the spoils of war past a cheering crowd. Only three major arches still survive in Rome—the arches of Constantine, Titus, and Septimius Severus (the last two are in the Forum)—but their continuing influence can be seen in London's Marble Arch and Paris's Arc de Triomphe.

ARCH OF CONSTANTINE

Triumphal arches, like celebratory columns, were usually raised as monuments to military achievement, in this case the victory of Constantine over his rival Maxentius at Milvian Bridge in AD 312 (making it one of the last great monuments to be built in ancient Rome). At 69 feet high and 85 feet wide it is the largest and best-preserved of the city's arches, and has recently been magnificently restored. Most of its reliefs were taken from earlier buildings, partly out of pragmatism and partly out of a desire to link Constantine's glories with those of the past. The battle scenes of the central arch show Trajan at war with the Dacians, while another describes a boar hunt and sacrifice to Apollo, carved in the time of Hadrian (2nd century AD).

✚ hIV, E6 ✉ Piazza del Colosseo-Via di San Gregorio, Via dei Fori Imperiali ⏰ Always open 🚇 Colosseo 🚌 11, 13, 15, 27, 30b, 81, 85, 87, 118, 186, 673 to Piazza del Colosseo ♿ Free

BATHS OF CARACALLA

Although the Terme di Caracalla were not the largest baths *(terme)* in ancient Rome (those of Diocletian near the present-day Piazza della Repubblica were bigger), the Baths of Caracalla were the city's most luxurious (and could accommodate as many as 1,600 bathers at one time). Started by Septimius Severus in AD 206, and completed by his son, Caracalla, 11 years later, they were designed as much for social meeting as for hygiene, since they were complete with gardens, libraries, sports facilities, stadiums, lecture rooms, shops— even hairdressers. They were open to both sexes, but bathing took place at different times. Something of the Terme's scale can still be gauged from today's ruins, although the site is perhaps now best known as the stage for outdoor opera in the summer (➤ 81).

✚ E8 ✉ Via delle Terme di Caracalla 52 ☎ 575 8626 ⏰ Tue–Sat 9AM to 2 hours before sunset; Sun, Mon 9–1. Closed public holidays 🚇 Circo Massimo 🚌 90, 90b, 118, 613, 617, 714, 715 to Piazzale Numa Pompilio ♿ Moderate

Carving from the Baths of Caracalla

CIRCUS MAXIMUS

Nestled in the natural hollow between the Palatine and Aventine Hills, this enormous grassy arena follows the outlines of a stadium capable of seating 300,000 people. Created to satisfy the passionate Roman appetite for chariot racing, and the prototype for almost all subsequent racecourses, it was begun around 326 BC and modified frequently before the occasion of its last recorded use under Totila the Ostrogoth in AD 549. Much of the original structure has long been quarried for building stone, but there remains the *spina* (the arena's old dividing wall), marked by a row of cypresses, the ruins of the imperial box, jutting out from the Palatine, and the open arena, now a public park (but one that should be avoided after dark).

🔲 D7 ✉ Via del Circo Massimo 🕐 Always open 🚇 Circo Massimo 🚌 11, 13, 15, 27, 30b, 90, 94, 118, 673 to Piazza di Porta Capena 🎫 Free

COLUMN OF MARCUS AURELIUS

The Column of Marcus Aurelius (AD 180–196) was built to celebrate Aurelius's military triumphs over hostile northern European tribes. Composed of 27 separate drums of Carraran marble, all cunningly welded into a seamless whole, the entire surface is covered with a continuous spiral of bas-reliefs commemorating episodes from the victorious campaigns. Aurelius is depicted no fewer than 59 times, though curiously never actually in battle. The summit statue does not depict a Roman at all, but St. Paul, crafted by Domenico Fontana in 1589 to replace the 60th depiction of Aurelius.

🔲 fII, D5 ✉ Piazza Colonna, Via del Corso 🕐 Always open 🚇 Barberini 🚌 56, 60, 85, 90, 90b, 119, 492 to Via del Corso 🎫 Free

TRAJAN'S MARKETS (*MERCATI TRAIANEI*)

Because of lack of space in the Roman Forum, the new Imperial Fora (Fori Imperiali) were begun in the 1st century BC by Julius Caesar and augmented by emperors Augustus, Vespasian, Nerva, and Trajan (the ruins of the buildings constructed during their rule are either side of the Via dei Fori Imperiali). Part of the largest, Trajan's Forum, was the Mercati Traianei, constructed at the beginning of the 2nd century AD as a semicircular range of halls on three levels. Two survive in excellent condition, together with many of the 150 booths that once traded rare and expensive commodities from all corners of the Empire. Look in particular at the Via Biberata, which took its name from *pipera* or pepper.

🔲 gIII, D6 ✉ Via IV Novembre 94 ☎ 6710 3613 🕐 Tue–Sat 9–1; Sun 9–12:30; Apr–Sep Thur, Sat 9–6. Closed Mon & public holidays 🚇 Cavour 🚌 57, 64, 65, 70, 75, 170 and other routes to Via IV Novembre 🎫 Moderate

At the races

Going to the races was as much a social event in ancient times as it is today. All types of people attended meetings, but different classes were kept rigidly separated. The emperor and his entourage sat on the imperial balcony, or *pulvinar*, while senators sat in the uppermost of the marble stalls. Lesser dignitaries occupied tiers of wooden seats, while the common rabble scrambled for standing room in open stands. The sexes, however, were unsegregated (unlike at the Coliseum), and the

Mercati Traianei, Trajan's Forum

races became notorious for their sexual license. Ovid recorded that at the Circo there was "no call for the secret language of fingers: nor need you depend on a furtive nod when you set upon a new affair."

MUSEUMS

John Keats

It was in what is now the Museo Keats–Shelley that the young English poet John Keats died on February 23, 1821, aged just 25. He had arrived in Rome the previous September, sent south to seek a cure for consumption. His time in Rome, however, he described as a "posthumous life," lamenting that he "already seemed to feel the flowers growing over him." (He was buried in the Protestant Cemetery ➤ 56).

See Top 25 Sights for
CAPITOLINE MUSEUMS ➤ 37
CASTEL SANT'ANGELO ➤ 27
GALLERIA BORGHESE ➤ 45
VATICAN MUSEUMS ➤ 25
VILLA GIULIA ➤ 35

MUSEO BARRACCO (PICCOLA FARNESINA)
This modest collection of Assyrian, Egyptian, Greek, Etruscan, and Roman artifacts is housed in the charming Piccola Farnesina, a miniature Renaissance palace.
elll, C6 ⊠ Corso Vittorio Emanuele II 166 ☎ 6880 6848 ⏰ Tue–Sun 9–1:30; Tue & Thu 5–8 🚍 46, 62, 64, 79, 81, 87, 90, 186, 492, 926 to Corso Vittorio Emanuele II 🚾 Moderate

MUSEO DEL FOLKLORE
Paintings, prints, and artifacts that illuminate the lives and times of past Romans.
C7 ⊠ Piazza Sant'Egidio 1, Trastevere ☎ 581 3717 ⏰ Tue–Sun 9–1; Tue and Thu 5–7.30 🚍 44, 56, 60, 75, 170, 181, 280, 717 to Piazza S Sonnino 🚾 Moderate

MUSEO DEL PALAZZO VENEZIA
Built in 1455 for Pietro Barbi (later Pope Paul II), the Palazzo Venezia was among the first Renaissance palaces in Rome. For years it was the Venetian Embassy (hence its name), becoming the property of the state in 1916. (Mussolini harangued the crowds from the balconies.) Today the museum hosts traveling exhibitions and a fine permanent collection that includes Renaissance paintings, sculpture, armor, ceramics, silverware, and countless *objets d'art*.
fIII, D6 ⊠ Palazzo Venezia, Via del Plebiscito 118 ☎ 679 8865 ⏰ Tue–Sat 9–2; Sun 9–1. Closed public holidays 🚍 All services to Piazza Venezia 🚾 Moderate

MUSEO KEATS–SHELLEY
Since 1909 this has been a museum and a library for students of Keats and Shelley, his fellow Romantic, both of whom died in Italy (see panel). Books, pamphlets, pictures, and essays lie scattered around the 18th-century house.
gI, D5 ⊠ Piazza di Spagna ☎ 678 4235 ⏰ Mon–Fri 9–1, 3–6 🚇 Spagna 🚍 119 to Piazza di Spagna 🚾 Moderate

MUSEO NAZIONALE ROMANO
Once one of the city's greatest museums, this state collection of ancient sculpture has an uncertain future. Its magnificent, but previously badly displayed collection of antiquities is to be rehoused in the Palazzo Massimo in Piazza dei Cinquecento.
E5 ⊠ Viale Enrico de Nicola 79 ☎ 4890 3507 ⏰ Tue–Sat 9–2; Sun 9–1 🚇 Repubblica 🚍 All services to Termini and Piazza dei Cinquecento 🚾 Moderate

Discobolus (the discus thrower)

ART GALLERIES

See Top 25 Sights for
PALAZZO BARBERINI ➤42
PALAZZO-GALLERIA DORIA PAMPHILI ➤36
PINACOTECA CAPITOLINA ➤37
PINACOTECA-MUSEI VATICANI ➤25
QUADERRIA DELLA GALLERIA BORGHESE AL
   SAN MICHELE A RIPA ➤45

GALLERIA DELL'ACCADEMIA NAZIONALE DI SAN LUCA

An interesting collection of 18th- and 19th-century paintings with earlier masterpieces by Raphael, Titian, Van Dyck, and Guido Reni.
➕ D5 ✉ Piazza dell'Accademia 77 ☎ 679 8850 ⏰ Mon, Wed, Fri, and the last Sun of every month 10–1 🚌 52, 53, 56, 58, 60, 61, 62, 71, 81, 95, 119 to Via del Tritone-Piazza Colonna 🎫 Free

PALAZZO CORSINI

Though in a separate building, this gallery is part of the Palazzo Barberini's Galleria Nazionale, housing later paintings from the national collection, with pictures by Rubens, Van Dyck, Murillo, and Caravaggio.
➕ dIV, C6 ✉ Via della Lungara 10 ☎ 6880 2323 ⏰ Tue–Sat 9–2; Sun and public holidays 9–1 🚌 23, 65, 280 to Lungotevere Farnesina 🎫 Moderate

PALAZZO-GALLERIA COLONNA

The best painting of this mostly 16th- to 18th-century (and rarely open) collection is Carracci's *Bean Eater*.
➕ gIII, D5 ✉ Via della Pilotta 17 ☎ 679 4362 ⏰ Sat only 9–1. Closed Sun–Fri and Aug 🚌 57, 64, 65, 70, 75, 81, 170, and other buses to Piazza Venezia 🎫 Moderate

PALAZZO SPADA

The pretty Palazzo Spada, with its creamy stucco façade (1556–1560), contains four rooms of paintings by Guido Reni, Guercino, Cerquozzi, Dürer, Andrea del Sarto, and others.
➕ eIII, C6 ✉ Piazza Capo di Ferro 13 ☎ 686 1158 ⏰ Tue–Sat 9–7; Sun 9–1 🍴 Café 🚌 44, 56, 60, 65, 75, 170, 181 to Via Arenula 🎫 Moderate

VILLA FARNESINA

This lovely Renaissance villa was completed in 1511 for Agostino Chigi (see panel) by Baldassare Peruzzi (and later sold to the Farnese). It is best known for the Loggia of Cupid and Psyche, decorated with frescoes (1517) by Raphael, for Sodoma's masterpiece, *Scenes from the Life of Alexander the Great*, and for the Salone delle Prospettive, Peruzzi's *trompe l'oeil* views of Rome.
➕ dIII, C6 ✉ Via della Lungara 230 ☎ 6880 1767 ⏰ Mon–Sat 9–1 🚌 23, 65, 280 to Lungotevere Farnesina 🎫 Free

A ceiling in the Villa Farnesina

Agostino Chigi

Agostino Chigi (d. 1512), from Siena, made his banking fortune by securing Rome's prize business —the papal account. He became renowned for flinging the family silver into the Tiber after gargantuan feasts at the Villa Farnesina. This bravura gesture of consumption was not all it seemed, however, for Chigi omitted to tell his admiring diners that a net strung below the water caught the loot for the next banquet.

53

FOUNTAINS

Fontana delle Naiadi

Fontana delle Naiadi

The Fountain of the Naiads in Piazza della Repubblica is of little historical or even of great artistic value. Nonetheless it is probably one of the most erotic works of art on public display anywhere in the world. Designed by Mario Rutelli, the sculptures were added in 1901. Water plays seductively over four frolicking and suggestively clad bronze nymphs, each entwined in the phallic-like tentacles of a marine creature so as to leave little to the imagination (each creature represents water in one of its forms—a swan for lakes, a sea-horse for the oceans, a water snake for rivers, and a lizard for underground streams).

See Top 25 Sights for FONTANA DI TREVI ►39.

FONTANA DELLE API

Small but captivating, Bernini's fountain was commissioned in honor of Pope Urban VIII, leading light of the Barberini clan. The fountain depicts a scallop shell, a symbol of life and fertility—a favorite Bernini conceit—at which three bees (*api*), taken from the Barberini coat-of-arms, have settled to drink.

➕ gI, E5 ✉ Piazza Barberini Ⓜ Barberini 🚌 52, 53, 56, 58, 60, 95, 119, 492 to Piazza Barberini

FONTANA DELLA BARCACCIA

This eccentric little fountain at the base of the Spanish Steps (►40)—translated literally it means the "Fountain of the Wretched Boat"—represents a half-sunken ship. Bernini was unable to create a greater aquatic display because of the low water pressure in the aqueduct feeding the fountain. Constructed in 1627–1629 by Pope Urban VIII, it is the work of Gian Lorenzo Bernini or his father Pietro.

➕ fI, D4/D5 ✉ Piazza di Spagna Ⓜ Spagna 🚌 119 to Piazza di Spagna

FONTANA DEL MORO

Designed in 1575 by Giacomo della Porta, the fountain at Piazza Navona's southern end shows a "Moor" (actually a marine divinity) grappling with a dolphin, a figure added by Antonio Mori from a design by Bernini.

➕ eII, C5 ✉ Piazza Navona 🚌 70, 81, 87, 90, 186, 492 to Corso del Rinascimento or 46, 62, 64 to Corso Vittorio Emanuele II

FONTANA PAOLA

The five arches and six granite columns of the monumental façade fronting this majestic fountain were built between 1610 and 1612 to carry the waters of Pope Paul's recently repaired Trajan Aqueduct. The columns were removed from the old St. Peter's, while many of the precious marbles were filched from the Temple of Minerva in the Imperial Fora.

➕ cIV, C6/C7 ✉ Via Garibaldi 🚌 41, 44, 75, 710 to the Gianicolo

FONTANA DEI QUATTRO FIUMI

Bernini's spirited "Fountain of the Four Rivers" at the heart of Piazza Navona was designed for Pope Innocent X in 1648 as part of a scheme to improve the approach to the Palazzo Doria Pamphili, and was unveiled in 1651. Its four figures represent the four rivers of Paradise, the Nile, Ganges, Danube, and Plate, and the four "corners" of the world, Africa,

Asia, Europe, and America. The dove atop the central obelisk is a symbol of the Pamphili family, of which Innocent was a member.

🕀 ell, C5 ⊠ Piazza Navona 🚌 70, 81, 87, 90, 186, 492 to Corso del Rinascimento or 46, 62, 64 to Corso Vittorio Emanuele II

FONTANA DELLE TARTARUGHE

This tiny creation is one of the most delightful sights in Rome, thanks largely to the tortoises added by Bernini in the 17th century to Giacomo della Porta's original 1585 fountain.

🕀 fIII, D6 ⊠ Piazza Mattei 🚌 44, 56, 60, 65, 75, 170, 181, 710, 718, 719 to Via Arenula

FONTANA DEL TRITONE

Like its companion piece the Fontana delle Api (► 54), the "Fountain of Triton" (1643) was also designed by Bernini for the Barberini pope Urban VIII. One of the sculptor's earliest fountains, the Fontana del Tritone is made of the then novel travertine, rather than the more usual marble. The fountain depicts four dolphins supporting twin scallop shells (bearing the Barberini coat-of-arms) on which the triumphant Triton is enthroned.

🕀 gl, E5 ⊠ Piazza Barberini 🚇 Barberini 🚌 52, 53, 56, 58, 60, 95, 119, 492 to Piazza Barberini

LE QUATTRO FONTANE

Recently cleaned, but reacquiring a patina of grime, these four linked fountains sit at a busy crossroads close to Via Nazionale. Built between 1585 and 1590, each contains a reclining deity—the two female figures are probably Juno and Diana (or Strength and Fidelity); the male figure the Nile or Aniene; and the last figure, shown with the she-wolf, a river god representing the Tiber.

🕀 hII, E5 ⊠ Via delle Quattro Fontane–Via del Quirinale 🚇 Repubblica 🚌 57, 64, 65, 70, 75, 81, 170 to Via Nazionale

Artistic rivalry

Well-worn Roman myths surround Bernini's Fontana dei Quattro Fiumi. One suggests the veiled figure of the Nile symbolizes the sculptor's dislike for the church of Sant'Agnese, designed by his fierce rival, Borromini (the veil actually symbolizes the river's unknown source). Another claims the figure representing the Plate is holding up his arm as if in horror of the church (either appalled by its design or afraid it is about to fall down). Sadly, neither myth is true, for Bernini finished the fountain before Borromini had even begun work on his church.

Fontana dei Quattro Fiumi

PARKS & GARDENS

The Protestant Cemetery

"...the cypress trees cast their long shadows upon the most extraordinary collection of exiles ever assembled in one place."
H. V. Morton, *A Traveller in Rome*

"The Cemetery is an open space among the ruins, covered in winter with violets and daisies. It might make one in love with death to know that one should be buried in so sweet a place." Percy Bysshe Shelley, Preface to *Adonis*

Via Appia Antica

BOTANICAL GARDENS (ORTO BOTANICO)

Trastevere has few open spaces, so these university gardens and their 7,000 or so botanical species—originally part of the Palazzo Corsini—provide a welcome slice of green shade.

➕ clV, C6 ✉ Largo Cristina di Svezia, off Via Corsini ☎ 686 4193 🕐 Mon–Sat 9–6 Closed Sun and public holidays 🚌 23, 65, 280 to Lungotevere Farnesina 🎟 Free

COLLE OPPIO

This homey area of park, once part of a palace complex built by Nero and redeveloped by Trajan, rests the eyes and feet after visits to the Colosseum, San Clemente or San Giovanni in Laterano.
A community meeting place, it's a welcoming mixture of grass and walkways (and wild cats), complete with promenading mothers, a small café and children's playground.

➕ hlV, E6 ✉ Via Labicana–Viale del Monte Oppio 🕐 Always open 🚌 11, 15, 16, 27, 81, 85 to Via Labicana 🎟 Free

PALATINE AND FARNESE GARDENS (*PALATINO E ORTI FARNESIANI*)

After a stroll around the Forum it's worth finding time to climb the Palatine Hill to enjoy a lovely garden haven. Orange groves, cypresses, and endless drowsy corners, all speckled with flowers and ancient stones, make up the Orti Farnesiani (Farnese Gardens), which were laid out over the ruins in the 16th century by the great Renaissance architect Vignola.

➕ glV, D6 ✉ Entrances from Via di San Gregorio and for the Roman Forum at Largo Romolo e Remo on Via dei Fori Imperiali ☎ 699 0110 🕐 Mon, Wed–Sat 9AM to 2 hours before sunset; Tue, Sun 9–2 🚇 Colosseo 🚌 11, 27, 81, 85, 87, 186 to Via dei Fori Imperiali 🎟 Expensive (includes entry to Roman Forum)

PARCO SAVELLO

Close to Santa Sabina (a lovely church in its own right), the Parco Savello is another little-known Roman park that lies closer to the center than you might expect. Its hilly position provides a lovely panorama over the Tiber and the city beyond.

➕ D7 ✉ Via Santa Sabina, Aventino 🕐 Dawn to dusk daily 🚌 94 🎟 Free

PINCIO GARDENS

Even if you cannot face the longer trip to the nearby Villa Borghese, be sure to walk to these gardens from Piazza del Popolo or Piazza di Spagna to enjoy the wonderful views (best at sunset) across the rooftops to St. Peter's.

➕ D4 ✉ Piazza del Pincio 🕐 Dawn to dusk daily 🚌 90, 90b, 95, 119, 926 to Piazzale Flaminio or Piazza del Popolo 🎟 Free

PROTESTANT CEMETERY (CIMITERO PROTESTANTE)

Described more than once as the "most beautiful cemetery in the world," this bucolic oasis is also something of a literary shrine, thanks to the graves of poets like John Keats, whose tombstone bears the epitaph "Here lies One whose Name was Writ in

Villa Doria Pamphili

Water" (see panel opposite). As late as the 19th century, burials here had to take place at night to avoid provoking attacks from outraged Catholics.

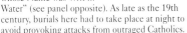 D8 ✉ Via Caio Cestio 6, Testaccio ☎ 574 1141 🕐 Mar–Sep, Thu–Tue 8–11:30, 3:20–5:30; Oct–Feb, 8–11:30, 2:20–4:30 🚌 13, 23, 27, 30b, 57, 94, 95, 716 to Piazza di Porta San Paolo 💷 Free but donation expected

VIA APPIA ANTICA

Once an imperial highway, this old roadway so close to the city center is now an evocative cobbled lane fringed with ancient monuments, tombs, catacombs, and lovely open country (see panel).

🕂 F9 ✉ Via Appia Antica 🕐 Always open 🚌 118 from the Colosseum, San Giovanni in Laterano, or the Terme di Caracalla 💷 Free

VILLA BORGHESE

Rome's largest central park was laid out as the grounds of the Borghese family's summer villa between 1613 and 1616. Smaller now, and redesigned in the 18th century to conform to the fashion for "English parkland," it still offers a shady retreat from the rigors of sightseeing. Walkways, woods, and lakes are complemented by fountains, a racetrack, children's playgrounds and a (rather tawdry) zoo.

🕂 D4/E4 ✉ Porta Pinciana–Via Flaminia 🕐 Dawn to dusk daily 🚇 Flaminio 🚌 3, 4, 52, 53, 57, 95, 490, 495, 910 💷 Free

VILLA CELIMONTANA

One of Rome's lesser-known parks, but easily accessible from the Colosseum and San Giovanni in Laterano.

🕂 E7 ✉ Piazza della Navicella 🕐 Daily 7–dusk 🚌 15, 673 to Via Claudia or 90, 90b to Via Druso 💷 Free

VILLA DORIA PAMPHILI

This huge area of parkland—laid out for Prince Camillo Pamphili in the mid-17th century—is probably too far from the center if you are just making a short visit to Rome. If you have time to spare, however, and fancy a good long walk away from the hordes, there is nowhere better.

🕂 A7 ✉ Via di San Pancrazio 🕐 Dawn to dusk daily 🚌 31, 41, 75, 144 to the Gianicolo 💷 Free

The Appia Antica

The Appia Antica was built in 312 BC by Appius Claudius Caecus to link Rome with Capua, and extended to Brindisi in 194 BC (320 miles and 13 days' march away). In 71 BC it was the spot where 6,000 of Spartacus's troops were crucified during a slaves' revolt. It sounded to the funeral processions of Sulla (78 BC) and Augustus (AD 14); it was the road along which St. Paul was marched as prisoner in AD 56; and close to the city walls was the point at which St. Peter (fleeing Rome) encountered Christ and, famously, asked him *"Domine, quo vadis?"* ("Lord, where are you going?").

MOSAICS

See Top 25 Sights for
SAN CLEMENTE ➤ 46
SAN GIOVANNI IN LATERANO ➤ 48
SANTA MARIA IN TRASTEVERE ➤ 28
SANTA MARIA MAGGIORE ➤ 47

Sant'Agnese (St. Agnes)

St. Agnes, who was martyred in Piazza Navona and buried near Sant'Agnese, was one of the most popular early Christian martyrs—despite the recorded fact that she failed to take a bath in the 13 years she was alive (such was her modesty). According to legend, this beautiful girl was martyred

Santa Prassede ceiling mosaics

for refusing to marry the son of a pagan governor of the city. For an earlier punishment she was thrown into a brothel. As she was about to be paraded naked, her hair grew miraculously to spare her blushes. Her steadfastness made her a symbol of Christian chastity, and her tomb became a place of pilgrimage particularly venerated by Roman women.

SANT'AGNESE FUORI LE MURA

Compare the outstanding Byzantine 7th-century mosaics in the apse of Sant'Agnese with the earlier mosaics in Santa Costanza (see below). The church was instigated in AD 342 by Constantia to be close to the tomb of the martyred Sant'Agnese (see panel). Although they were rather clumsily restored in 1855, the mosaics survive intact, showing Agnes, with the sword of her martyrdom at her feet, flanked by the 7th-century rebuilder Pope Honorius I.

🚇 G3 ✉ Via Nomentana 349 ☎ 861 0840 🕐 Mon–Sat 9–12, 4–6; Sun 4–6 🚌 36, 36b, 37, 60, 136, 137 to Via Nomentana–Via di Santa Costanza 🎟 Free

SANTA COSTANZA

In the church, originally built as a mausoleum for Constantia and Helena (daughters of the Emperor Constantine), are exquisite 4th-century mosaics. Note their white background, in contrast to the gold in Byzantine work of later centuries. Note, too, the pagan icons adapted to Christian use—especially the lamb and peacock, symbols of innocence and immortality respectively.

🚇 G3 ✉ Via Nomentana 349 ☎ 861 0840 🕐 Mon, Wed–Sat 9–12, 4–6; Sun 4–6 🚌 36, 36b, 37, 60, 136, 137 to Via Nomentana–Via di Santa Costanza 🎟 Cheap

SANTA MARIA IN DOMNICA AND SANTO STEFANO ROTONDO

Like those in Santa Prassede, the glorious mosaics in the apse of Santa Maria in Domnica 9th-century church were commissioned by Pope Paschal I, who is shown at the foot of the Virgin and Child and a host of adoring angels (his square halo indicates he was alive when the mosaic was made). Almost opposite Santa Maria in Domnica, stands Santo Stefano Rotondo, one of whose chapels boasts a 7th-century mosaic commemorating two martyrs buried nearby. The church also contains some eye-opening frescoes, grisly tableaux of martyrdoms (see panel).

🚇 E7 ✉ Piazza della Navicella 12 and Via di Santo Stefano 7 ☎ 700 1519; Santo Stefano 7049 3717 🕐 Daily 8:30–12, 3:30–6. Santo Stefano Mon–Fri 9–12 🚌 15, 673 to Via della Navicella 🎟 Free

SANTA PRASSEDE

The treasure of this church is the stunning mosaic work, commissioned by Pope Paschal I in 822 to decorate his mother's mausoleum in the Cappella di San Zeno. So beautiful were the mosaics that in the Middle Ages the gold-encrusted chapel became known as the Garden of Paradise. Similar Byzantine mosaics adorn the church's apse and triumphal arch.

➕ E6 ✉ Via Santa Prassede 9a ☎ 488 2456 🕐 Daily 7:30–12, 4–6:30 🚌 11, 27 to Via Cavour-Piazza Esquilino 🎟 Free

SANTA PUDENZIANA

Built in the 4th century (but much altered over the years), this church was reputedly raised over the house of the Roman senator Pudens, site of St. Peter's conversion of the senator's daughters, Pudenziana and Prassede (see above). Its prized apse mosaic dates from this period, an early-Christian depiction of a golden-robed Christ, the apostles, and two women, presumed to be Prassede and Pudenziana.

➕ hII, E5 ✉ Via Urbana 160 ☎ 481 4622 🕐 Daily 8–12, 4–7 (Oct–Mar 3–6PM) 🚇 Termini 🚌 70, 71 to Via A de Pretis or 11, 27 to Via Cavour-Piazza Esquilino 🎟 Free

SANTI COSMA E DAMIANO

This church is housed in part of the former Forum of Vespasian, one of the Imperial Fora, though its rebuilding in 1632 wiped out all but a few vestiges of its original classical and medieval splendor. Chief of the surviving treasures is the magnificent 6th-century Byzantine mosaic in the apse, a work that influenced Roman and other mosaicists for centuries to come.

➕ gIV, D6 ✉ Via dei Fori Imperiali ☎ 699 1540 🕐 Daily 7–1, 3–7 🚌 All routes to Piazza Venezia and 11, 27, 81, 85, 87, 186 to Via Fori Imperiali 🎟 Free

Mosaics in Capella di San Zeno, Santa Prassede

Santo Stefano's frescoes

"...hideous paintings...such a panorama of horror and butchery no man could imagine in his sleep, though he were to eat a whole pig, raw, for his supper. Grey-bearded men being boiled, fried, crimped, singed, eaten by wild beasts, worried by dogs, buried alive, torn asunder by horses, chopped up small with hatchets; women having their breasts torn off with iron pincers, their tongues cut out, their ears screwed off, their jaws broken, their bodies stretched on the rack, or skinned on the stake, or crackled up and melted in the fire — these are among the mildest subjects." Charles Dickens, *Pictures from Italy*

Mosaics in Santa Prassede

59

CHURCHES

SANTA MARIA DELLA CONCEZIONE

Rome's most ghoulish sight lurks behind an unassuming façade in the unlikely surroundings of the Via Vittorio Veneto. Lying in the crypt of Santa Maria della Concezione are the remains of 4,000 Capuchin monks, some still dressed in jaunty clothes, the bones of others crafted into macabre chandeliers and bizarre wall decorations. The bodies were originally buried in soil especially imported from Jerusalem. When this ran out they were left uncovered, a practice that continued until 1870. The church was built in 1624 by Cardinal Antonio Barberini, brother of Urban VIII, a Capuchin friar who lies buried before the main altar under a cheerful legend: "*hic jacet pulvis cinis et nihil*" ("here lie dust, ashes, and nothing"). The church is known for Guido Reni's painting *St. Michael Tempting the Devil*, in which the Devil is reputedly a portrait of the Pamphili Pope Innocent X.

➕ gI, E5 ✉ Via Vittorio Veneto 27 ☎ 487 1185 ⏰ **Church** Daily 7–12, 4–7 **Crypt** (Cimitero dei Cappuccini) Daily 9–12, 3–6 🚌 52, 53, 56, 58, 58b, 490, 495, and others to Via V Veneto 🎫 **Church** Free **Crypt** Donation

SANTA MARIA IN COSMEDIN

This lovely old medieval church—one of the most atmospheric in the city—is best known for the Bocca della Verità, a weatherbeaten stone face (of the seagod Oceanus) once used by the ancient Romans as a drain cover (see panel). Inside, the church has a beautiful pavement, twin *ambos*, or pulpits, a bishop's throne, and a stone choir screen, all decorated in fine Cosmati stone inlay. Most date from the 12th century, a little earlier than the impressive *baldacchino*, or altar canopy, built by Deodato di Cosma in 1294. Tucked away in a small room off the right aisle is a mosaic of the *Adoration of the Magi*, almost all that remains of an 8th-century Greek church on the site.

➕ D7 ✉ Piazza della Bocca della Verità ☎ 678 1419 ⏰ Daily 9–12, 3–5 🚌 15, 23, 57, 90, 92, 94, 95, 160, 716 to Piazza Bocca della Verità 🎫 Free

Santa Maria in Cosmedin

La Bocca della Verità

The *bocca* of the "Mouth of Truth" is a gaping marble mouth. Anyone suspected of lying—particularly women accused of adultery—would have his or her right hand forced into the maw. Legend says that, in the case of dissemblers, the mouth would clamp shut and sever their fingers. To give credence to the story a priest supposedly hid behind the stone to hit the fingers of those known to be guilty.

ROME
where to...

EXPENSIVE RESTAURANTS

You can expect to pay L50,000 or more, excluding wine, in this category of restaurant.

Change of career

According to a legend—whose origins are now some 25 years old—La Rosetta's famous owner, the Sicilian Carmelo Riccioli, abandoned a career as a boxer and a sports writer when he won this restaurant as payment for a bet.

ALBERTO CIARLA

Rome's best fish restaurant with a fine wine list. The food is elegantly presented, to go with the candlelit ambience and impeccable service.
⊕ C7 ⊠ Piazza San Cosimato 40 ☎ 581 8668 ⏰ Mon–Sat 12:30–3; 8:30–11:30. Closed 15 days in Aug, Christmas, and 15 days in Jan 🚌 44, 75, 170, 181, 280, 717 to Viale di Trastevere

CHECCHINO DAL 1887

Robust appetites are required for this menu. Quintessential Roman dishes (awarded one Michelin star), relying largely on offal are its specialty. Reservations recommended.
⊕ C8/D8 ⊠ Via Monte Testaccio 30 ☎ 574 3816 ⏰ Tue–Sat 12:30–3, 8:30–11; Sun–Mon 12:30–3PM. Closed Aug and Christmas 🚌 13, 23, 27, 57, 95, 716 to Piramide and Via Marmorata

DA PATRIZIA E ROBERTO DEL PIANETA TERRA

Perfect for a relaxed and intimate evening, and on the second floor of a 14th-century *palazzo*. The top-rate cooking is light, modern, and inventive. It's best to reserve ahead.
⊕ eIII, C6 ⊠ Via dell'Arco del Monte 94–5 ☎ 6880 1663 ⏰ Tue–Sun 12:30–3, 8–11. Closed Mon & Aug 🚌 44, 56, 60, 65, 75, 170, 181, 710 to Via Arenula

EL TOULÀ

Considered by many Rome's best restaurant, the food is inspired by a mixture of Venetian and International cuisine.

Service is formal, in keeping with the restaurant's traditional atmosphere.
⊕ el, D5 ⊠ Via della Lupa 29b ☎ 687 3498 ⏰ Mon–Fri 1–3, 8–11; Sat 8–11PM. Closed Aug and Christmas 🚌 81, 90 to Via del Corso-Largo Carlo Goldini

IL CONVIVIO

The Troiani brothers from Italy's Marche region have created a tranquil and urbane little restaurant (one Michelin star) with a reputation for innovative and subtly flavored modern dishes.
⊕ ell, C5 ⊠ Via dell'Orso 44 ☎ 686 9432 ⏰ Mon–Sat 12:30–2:30, 7:30–11. Closed May 🚌 70, 81, 90, 90b, 186 to Ponte Umberto-Lungotevere Marzio

LA ROSETTA

An exclusive fish and seafood restaurant whose popularity means booking is a must (see panel). Has one Michelin star.
⊕ ell, D5 ⊠ Via della Rosetta 9 ☎ 6830 8841 ⏰ Mon–Sat 1–3, 8–11:30. Closed 3 weeks in Aug and Christmas 🚌 119 to Piazza della Rotonda or 70, 81, 87, 90 to Corso del Rinascimento

SABATINI

Once Rome's most famous restaurant, Sabatini is still popular for its reliable food in a lovely setting, though prices are higher than the cooking deserves. Reservations essential.
⊕ dIV, C6 ⊠ Piazza Santa Maria in Trastevere 13 (and Vicolo Santa Maria in Trastevere 18) ☎ 581 2026 (and 581 8307) ⏰ Mon, Tue, Thu–Sun 12–2:30; 7:30–11 Closed Wed and Aug 🚌 44, 56, 60, 75, 170, 181, 280 to Piazza S. Sonnino

MID-PRICE RESTAURANTS

AL MORO
Fellini's favorite restaurant in the 1960s. A rambunctious busy trattoria near the Fontana di Trevi (in an alley off Via delle Muratte) with close tables and good traditional cooking. Reservation essential.
➕ fII, D5 ✉ Vicolo delle Bollette 13 ☎ 678 3495 🕐 Mon–Sat 12:30–3, 7:30–11. Closed Aug 🚌 56, 60, 62, 85, 90, 160 to Via del Corso

AL 34
Popular, award-winning and known for its Roman and southern Italian-based cooking, and for its romantic and candlelit intimacy. Close to Via Condotti and the Spanish Steps. Reservation recommended.
➕ fIV, D6 ✉ Via Mario de' Fiori 34 ☎ 679 5091 🕐 Tue–Sun 12:30–3, 7:30–11. Closed 3 weeks in Aug 🚇 Spagna 🚌 119

NERONE
A small, old-fashioned trattoria best known for its buffet of antipasti and simple Abruzzese cooking. Outside tables.
➕ hIV, E6 ✉ Via delle Terme di Tito 96 ☎ 474 5207 🕐 Mon–Sat 12:30–2:30, 7:30–10:30. Closed Aug 🚌 11, 13, 27, 30, 81, 85, 87, 186 to Piazza del Colosseo

PARIS
An extremely popular and elegant little restaurant in Trastevere known for its fish, pastas, and the quality of its Roman-based cooking. Outside tables. Reservations are essential.
➕ dIV, C7 ✉ Piazza San Callisto 7a ☎ 581 5378 🕐 Tue–Sat 12:30–3, 8–11; Sun 12:30–3. Closed 3 weeks in Aug 🚌 44, 56, 60, 75, 170, 181, 280, 717 to Piazza San Sonnino

PIERLUIGI
A perennial favorite with locals, expats, celebrities, and visitors especially Sunday at lunchtime. Outside tables.
➕ dIII, C6 ✉ Piazza dei Ricci 144/Via Monserrato ☎ 686 8717 🕐 Tue–Sun 12:30–2:30, 7:30–10 🚌 46, 62, 64 to Corso Vittorio Emanuele II

ROMOLO
This is a long-established fixture in Trastevere, housed in what was reputedly the home of Raphael's model and mistress, the "Fornarina" (baker's daughter). An outside courtyard is candlelit for dinner.
➕ dIV, C7 ✉ Via Porta Settimiana 8 ☎ 581 8284 🕐 Tue–Sun 12:30–2:30, 7:30–11:30. Closed 3 weeks in Aug 🚌 23, 65, 280 to Lungotevere Farnesina

VECCHIA ROMA
In a pretty piazza on the edge of the Ghetto and perfect for an *al fresco* meal on a summer evening, though the 18th-century interior is also captivating. Prices are high, however, for what is only straightforward and reliable Roman cooking.
➕ fIV, D6 ✉ Piazza Campitelli 18 ☎ 686 4604 🕐 Mon, Tue, Thu–Sun 1–3, 8–11 🚌 44, 46, 56, 60, 75, 85, 87, 94 and all other services to Piazza Venezia

Expect to pay L30,000–50,000 without wine for a meal in a mid-price restaurant.

Roman specialties

Roman favorites— though they are by no means confined to the city— include pastas like *bucatini all'Amatriciana* (tomato sauce, salt pork, and chilli peppers); *spaghetti alla carbonara* (egg, bacon, pepper, and cheese); and *gnocchi alla Romana* (small potato or semolina dumplings with tomato or butter). The best-known main course is *saltimbocca alla Romana* (veal escallops with ham and sage, cooked in wine and butter). Less familiar perhaps to tourists but nevertheless traditional are *trippa* (tripe), *cervelli* (brains) and *coda alla vaccinara* (oxtail).

BUDGET RESTAURANTS

Meals in a budget restaurant may cost anything up to L30,000, without wine.

Menus

If no menu is offered, ask for *la lista* or *il menù*. A set-price menu (*un menù turistico*) may seem good value, but portions are small and the food is invariably poor—usually just spaghetti with a tomato sauce and a piece of chicken with fruit to follow. Starters are called *antipasti*; first course (soup, pasta, or risotto) is *il primo*; and main meat and fish dishes are *il secondo*. Salads (*insalata*) and vegetables (*contorni*) are ordered (and often eaten) separately. Desserts are *dolci*, with cheese (*formaggio*) or fruit (*frutta*) to follow.

AUGUSTO

One of the last remaining cheap and authentic family-run trattorias in Trastevere.
⊞ dIV, C6 ✉ Piazza de' Renzi 15 ☎ 580 3798 🕔 Mon–Sat 12:30–3, 7:30–11. Closed Aug 🚌 23, 65, 280 to Lungotevere Sanzio or 44, 56, 60, 75, 170 to Piazza S. Sonnino

BIRRERIA FRATELLI TEMPERA

Close to Piazza Venezia for a simple lunch or early evening meal. Original art nouveau interior. A large and easy-going beer-hall atmosphere. Especially busy at lunchtimes.
⊞ fII, D5 ✉ Via di San Marcello 19 ☎ 678 6203 🕔 Mon–Sat 12:30–2:45, 7:30–11 🚌 44, 46, 64, 75, 85, 87, 94 and all other buses to Piazza Venezia

CRISCIOTTI

Confirms the theory that the worse the paintings in a Roman trattoria, the better the food. Pleasant and pretty with affable service. Mushroom and fresh fish specialties.
⊞ hIII, E6 ✉ Via del Boschetto 30 ☎ 474 4770 🕔 Mon–Fri, Sun 12:30–3, 7–11. Closed Aug 🚇 Cavour 🚌 57, 64, 65, 70, 75, 81, 170 to Via Nazionale

DA LUCIA

Tiny and basic Trastevere hideaway. The Roman atmosphere and local cooking are first rate. Outdoor tables.
⊞ dIV, C6 ✉ Via del Mattonato 2b ☎ 580 3601 🕔 Tue–Sun 12:30–2:30, 7:30–11. Closed 3 weeks in Aug 🚌 23, 65, 280 to Lungotevere Farnesina or 44, 56, 60, 75, 170 to Piazza S. Sonnino

DA VALENTINO

A tiny and unassuming old-fashioned Roman trattoria close to the Forum.
⊞ hIII, E6 ✉ Via Cavour 293 ☎ 488 1303 🕔 Mon–Thu, Sat, Sun 12–3, 7–10 🚇 Cavour 🚌 11, 27, 81 to Via Cavour or 85, 87, 186 to Via dei Fori Imperiali

FIASCHETTERIE BELTRAMME DA CESARETTO

In a historical monument, with a fine outside courtyard. Inside, shared tables have a bustling atmosphere. Convenient to the Spanish Steps.
⊞ fI, D5 ✉ Via della Croce 39 ☎ No phone 🕔 Mon–Sat 12:15–3, 7:30–11. Closed 2 weeks in Aug 🚇 Spagna 🚌 119 to Piazza di Spagna or 81, 90 to Via del Corso

FILETTI DI BACCALÀ

At this tiny place with Formica tables close to Campo de' Fiori, filets of cod (and little else) are washed down with beer or drafts of crisp local wine.
⊞ eIII, C6 ✉ Largo dei Librari 88, off Via dei Giubbonari ☎ No phone 🕔 Mon–Sat 12:30–2:30, 7–10:30 🚌 44, 56, 60, 65, 75, 170, 181, 710, 718, 719 to Via Arenula

MARIO ALLA VITE

Simple Tuscan cooking served in a crowded and slightly chaotic restaurant. Convenient for the Via Condotti and the Spanish Steps.
⊞ fI, D5 ✉ Via della Vite 55 ☎ 678 3818 🕔 Mon–Sat 12:30–3, 7:30–11. Closed Aug 🚇 Spagna 🚌 119 to Piazza di Spagna

PIZZERIAS

BAFFETTO ($)

Rome's most famous pizzeria. A tiny, hole-in-the wall classic that has retained its atmosphere and low prices despite its fame. Expect lines.

🕂 dII, C5 ⊠ Via del Governo Vecchio 11 ☎ 686 1617 🕔 Mon–Sat 6:30PM–12:45AM 🚌 46, 62, 64 to Corso Vittorio Emanuele II

CORALLO ($)

Rather up-scale, this popular and occasionally chaotic pizzeria is convenient for Piazza Navona. Full meals are also available.

🕂 dII, C5 ⊠ Via del Corallo 10, off Via del Governo Vecchio ☎ 6830 7703 🕔 Mon–Sat 7:30PM–1:30AM. Closed 1 week in Aug. 🚌 46, 62, 64 to Corso Vittorio Emanuele II

DA VITTORIO ($)

Tiny Neapolitan-run Trastevere pizzeria that makes a good standby if Ivo is busy.

🕂 C7 ⊠ Via di San Cosimato 14a, Piazza San Callisto ☎ 580 0353 🕔 Mon–Sat 7PM–12 🚌 44, 56, 60, 75, 170, 181, 280, 717 to Viale di Trastevere

EST! EST! EST! ($)

Among the oldest pizzerias in Rome; worth the slight walk if you are around Stazione Termini.

🕂 hII, E5 ⊠ Via Genova 32 ☎ 488 1107 🕔 Tue–Sun 6:30–11:30PM. Closed mid-Aug 🚇 Repubblica 🚌 57, 64, 65, 70, 71, 75, 170 to Via Nazionale

IVO ($)

The best-known and most authentic of Trastevere's pizzerias.

Lines are common but turnover is quick.

🕂 C7 ⊠ Via di San Francesco a Ripa 158 ☎ 581 7082 🕔 Mon, Wed–Sun 7PM–1AM . Closed 3 weeks in Aug 🚌 44, 56, 60, 75, 170, 181, 280, 717 to Viale di Trastevere

LA CAPRICCIOSA ($)

Reputedly the birthplace of the *capricciosa* pizza. A full restaurant service pizzeria (though pizzas are only available at dinner). Boasts a roomy, rather stylish dining room, plus a terrace for *al fresco* eating.

🕂 fI, D5 ⊠ Largo dei Lombardi 8, Via del Corso ☎ 687 8480 🕔 Mon, Wed–Sun 12:15AM–3PM, 7PM–12:30AM. Closed 3 weeks in Aug 🚇 Spagna 🚌 81, 90, 119 to Via del Corso–Via della Croce

LEONCINO ($)

Nothing has changed in the wonderful old-fashioned interior for over 30 years. Authentic food and atmosphere. Popular, so expect a line. Open at lunch.

🕂 fI, D5 ⊠ Via del Leoncino 28, Piazza San Lorenzo in Lucina ☎ 687 6306 🕔 Mon–Fri 1–2:30PM, 7PM–12 ; Sat 7PM–12 🚇 Spagna 🚌 81, 90, 119 to Via del Corso-Via Tomacelli

PANATTONI ($)

Big, bright, and often busy place known locally as L'Obitorio (The Morgue) on account of its cold marble tables. Tables outside on Viale di Trastevere.

🕂 eIV, C7 ⊠ Viale di Trastevere 53 ☎ 580 0919 🕔 Mon, Tue, Thu–Sun 7PM–1AM. Closed 3 weeks in Aug 🚌 44, 56, 60, 75, 170, 181, 280, 717 to Viale di Trastevere

The check

The check is *il conto* and usually includes extras such as cover (*pane e coperto*) and service (*servizio*). Proper checks—not a scrawled piece of paper—must be given by law. If you receive a scrap of paper—and you are more likely to in a pizzeria—and have doubts about the total be sure to ask for *una fattura*.

65

ETHNIC & INTERNATIONAL RESTAURANTS

Unusual waitresses

You are served at the L'Eau Vive by nuns from a Third World order known as the Vergini Laiche Cristiane di Azione Cattolica Missionaria per Mezzo del Lavoro (Christian Virgins of Catholic Missionary Action though Work). With restaurants in several parts of the world, their aim is to spread the message of Christianity through the medium of French food. To this end dining is interrupted by prayers each evening at 9PM.

AFRICA ($)

A long-established restaurant close to Termini catering mainly to Rome's Ethiopian and Eritrean population.
➕ F5 ⬛ Via Gaeta 26 ☎ 494 1077 🕐 Tue–Sun 9AM–1PM. Closed 2 weeks in Aug 🚌 38, 57, 319 to Via Volturno and all buses to Termini

BIRRERIA VIENNESE ($)

An authentic Austrian beer house with a wide range of beers and Austro-German specialties.
➕ fI, D5 ⬛ Via della Croce 21 ☎ 679 5569 🕐 Mon, Tue, Thu–Sun 🚇 Spagna 🚌 81, 90 to Via del Corso or 119 to Piazza di Spagna

CHARLY'S SAUCIÈRE ($$)

Well-established restaurant offering reliable French and Swiss staples in a cozy setting.
➕ hIV, F7 ⬛ Via di San Giovanni in Laterano 270 ☎ 704 94700 🕐 Mon–Sat 8PM–12. Closed 2 weeks in Aug 🚌 85 to Via San Giovanni in Laterano

GEORGE'S ($$$)

One of the city's leading restaurants, established 50 years ago, though the splendor of its *dolce vita* heyday is now slightly faded. Good but rarely exceptional French, Italian and international cuisine. Polished service and a refined and elegant ambience. Jacket, tie, and reservations essential.
➕ E4 ⬛ Via Marche 7 ☎ 474 5204 🕐 Mon–Sat 12:30–3, 7:30PM–1AM. Closed Aug 🚇 Spagna 🚌 52, 53, 56, 58, 95 to Via Vittorio Veneto

GIGGETTO ($)

Another famous Romano-Jewish restaurant in the Ghetto district, it comes a close (and slightly cheaper) second to the Piperno.
➕ fIV, D6 ⬛ Via Portico d'Ottavia 21a ☎ 686 1105 🕐 Tue–Sun 12:30–2:30, 7:30–10:30 🚌 44, 56, 60, 65, 75, 170, 181, 710, 718, 719 to Via Arenula

L'EAU VIVE ($$–$$$)

A pleasantly bizarre dining experience. The (predominantly) French food is served by nuns (see panel). Politicians, celebrities, and locals alike come to enjoy the food, the ambience, and the beautiful 16th-century frescoed dining rooms.
➕ eIII, D6 ⬛ Via Monterone 85 ☎ 654 1095 or 6880 1095 🕐 Mon–Sat 12:30–3:30, 7:30–10. Closed first week of Aug 🚌 44, 46, 56, 60, 61, 64, 65, 70, 75, 81, 87, 90, 170 to Largo di Torre Argentina

PIPERNO ($$)

Much Roman cuisine is based on the city's extensive Jewish culinary traditions. The famous and resolutely traditional Piperno has been a temple to Romano-Jewish cuisine for over a century. Be sure to book well ahead.
➕ eIV, D6 ⬛ Via Monte de' Cenci 9 ☎ 6880 6629 or 6880 2772 🕐 Tue–Sat 12:15–3, 7:30–10:30; Sun 12:15–3. Closed Aug, Christmas and Easter 🚌 44, 56, 60, 65, 75, 170, 181, 710, 718, 719 to Via Arenula

ICE CREAM PARLORS

ALBERTO PICA

Only 20 flavors, but of excellent quality; try the house specialties like green apple (*mele verde*) and Sicilian citrus (*agrumi di Sicilia*).
🔲 eIV, C6 🖂 Via della Seggiola 12 (off Via Arenula opposite Piazza Cenci) ☎ 688 03275 ⏰ Mon–Sat 8AM–1AM 🚍 44, 56, 60, 65, 75, 170, 181, 710, 718, 719 to Via Arenula

DA MIRELLA

Sells *Granita*, crushed ice drenched in juice or syrup. In this kiosk, the flavorings are based on years of experience; the ice is still hand ground.
🔲 eIV, D6 🖂 Lungotevere Anguillara, Ponte Cestio ☎ No phone ⏰ Daily 8AM–late 🚍 23, 717, 774, 780

GELATERIA DELLA PALMA

A big, brash place behind the Pantheon. Cakes and chocolates, plus over 100 flavors of ice cream—many of them wild and wonderful.
🔲 eII, D5 🖂 Via della Maddalena 20 ☎ 654 0752 ⏰ Thu–Tue noon to midnight 🚍 119 to Piazza della Rotonda

GIOLITTI

For years the king of Roman ice cream. Standards have slipped slightly, but the ice cream, coffee, and cakes are still of excellent value.
🔲 fII, D5 🖂 Via Uffici del Vicario 40 ☎ 699 1243 ⏰ Tue–Fri, Sun 7AM–12:30AM; Sat 7AM–2AM 🚍 119 to Piazza della Rotonda or 52, 53, 56, 60, 62, 81, 85, 90, 160 to Via del Corso

LA FONTE DELLA SALUTE

At the so-called "Fount of Health" ice creams are made with fresh cream, sugar, eggs, and other far from healthy ingredients.
🔲 C7 🖂 Via Cardinale Marmaggi 2–6 ☎ No phone ⏰ Tue–Sun 8AM–1OPM 🚍 44, 56, 60, 75, 170, 181, 280 to Viale di Trastevere

PREMIATE GELATERIE FANTASIA

A good port-of-call near the church of San Giovanni in Laterano.
🔲 G7 🖂 Via La Spezia 100–2 ☎ No phone 🚇 San Giovanni ⏰ Mon–Sat 8AM–11PM 🚇 San Giovanni 🚍 4, 13, 16, 30, 81, 85, 87 to Piazzale Appio

SACCHETTI

Family-run bar also good for cakes and pastries.
🔲 C7 🖂 Piazza San Cosimato 62 ☎ 581 5374 ⏰ Tue–Sun 5AM–1OPM 🚍 44, 75, 170, 181, 280, 717 to Viale di Trastevere

SAN FILIPPO

This quiet-looking bar in Parioli is for many the best *gelateria* in the city. Zabaglione is emperor of the 60-odd flavors.
🔲 E2 🖂 Via di Villa San Filippo 8–10 ☎ 807 9314 ⏰ Tue–Sun 7:30AM–11:30PM 🚍 3, 19, 30, 53, 168 to Piazza Ungheria or 4 to Via di Villa San Filippo

TRE SCALINI

Celebrated for its chocolate-studded *tartufo*, the ultimate in chocolate chip ice cream.
🔲 eII, C5 🖂 Piazza Navona 28–32 ☎ 6880 1996 ⏰ Thu–Tue 8AM–1AM 🚍 70, 81, 87, 90, 186, 492 to Corso del Rinascimento

Buying ice cream

Ice cream in a proper *gelateria* is sold either in a cone (*un cono*) or a paper cup (*una coppa*). Specify which you want and then decide how much you wish to pay: sizes of cone and cup go up in lire bands, usually starting small and ending enormous. You can choose up two or three flavors (more in bigger tubs) and will usually be asked if you want a twirl of cream (*panna*) to round things off.

BARS BY DAY

Bar etiquette

You almost always pay a premium to sit down (inside or outside) and to enjoy the privilege of waiter service in Roman bars. If you stand—which is cheaper— the procedure is to pay for what you want first at the cash-desk (*la cassa*). You then take your receipt (*lo scontrino*) to the bar and repeat your order (a tip slapped down on the bar will work wonders in attracting the bar-person's attention). Pastry shops, coffee bars, and ice cream parlors often double as excellent all-around bars to be enjoyed during the day. They include Giolitti and Tre Scalini (► 67), and Camilloni, Sant'Eustachio, and Bernasconi (► 69).

ALEMAGNA

This big century-old bar has a huge and varied passing trade. Good self-service selection of hot and cold food.
➕ fl, D5 ⊠ Via del Corso 181 ☎ 678 9135 🕐 Mon—Sat 7:30AM—11PM 🚇 Spagna 🚌 119 to Piazza Augusto Imperatore

BAR DELLA PACE

Extremely trendy, but quieter by day, when you can sit outside or enjoy the mirror-and-mahogany 19th-century interior .
➕ ell, C5 ⊠ Via della Pace 3, off Piazza Navona ☎ 686 1216 🕐 Tue—Sun 9AM—2AM 🚌 70, 81, 87, 90, 186, 492 to Corso del Rinascimento

CANOVA

Canova is pricier and less atmospheric than Rosati, though its sunny outside tables provide a welcome pause for the feet.
➕ D4 ⊠ Piazza del Popolo 16 ☎ 361 2231 🕐 Daily 7:30AM—12:30AM 🚇 Flaminio or Spagna 🚌 119 to Piazza del Popolo

CASINA VALADIER

Join the chatting Roman matrons and their dogs on the terrace bar of this neoclassical folly over-looking the city.
➕ D4 ⊠ Piazzale Napoleone, Viale Valadier, Pincio ☎ 6992 0264 🕐 Tue—Sat 10AM—noon, 8—12PM 🚇 Spagna 🚌 119 to Piazza del Popolo

CIAMPINI

You can sit here for hours facing Bernini's Fontana dei Quattro Fiumi (► 54) but watch the prices.
➕ ell, C5 ⊠ Piazza Navona 94—100 ☎ 686 1547

🕐 Tue—Sun 8:30AM—12:30AM 🚌 46, 62, 64 to Corso Vittorio Emanuele II or 70, 81, 87, 90, 186, 492 to Corso del Rinascimento

DONEY

Most of the bars famous in the *dolce vita* days of the 1950s are now tacky and expensive. But Doney is as tasteful and inviting as ever.
➕ gl, E5 ⊠ Via Vittorio Veneto 145 ☎ 482 1788 🕐 Tue—Sat 8AM—1AM 🚇 Barberini 🚌 52, 53, 56, 58, 95 to Via Vittorio Veneto

LATTERIA DEL GALLO

Old-fashioned, with original marble tables and 1940s décor in an alley between Campo de' Fiori and Piazza Farnese. Try big, sticky cakes and steaming bowls of hot chocolate.
➕ dll, C6 ⊠ Vicolo del Gallo 4 ☎ 686 5091 🕐 Thu—Tue 9—1, 5:30—11:30 🚌 46, 62, 64 to Corso Vittorio Emanuele II

ROSATI

Wonderful coffee, cock-tails, cakes, and pastries (from 70-year-old ovens) and a glittering 1922 art nouveau interior.
➕ D4 ⊠ Piazza del Popolo 5 ☎ 322 5859 🕐 Wed—Mon 7:30AM—11:30PM 🚇 Flaminio or Spagna 🚌 119 to Piazza del Popolo

TRASTÈ

This trendy tea and coffee shop in Trastevere also serves light meals. People come to chat, read newspapers and lounge away the time.
➕ elV, C6 ⊠ Via della Lungaretta 76 ☎ 589 4430 🕐 Tue—Sun 4PM—1AM 🚌 44, 56, 60, 75, 170, 181, 280, 717 to Piazza S. Sonnino

CUPS OF COFFEE & CAKE SHOPS

ANTICO CAFFÈ BRASILE

Beans and ground coffee are sold from vast sacks; there is also a superb variety of coffees at the bar. Try the "Pope's blend": John Paul II bought his coffee here before becoming pontiff.
🚼 hlll, E6 ⊠ Via dei Serpenti 23 ☎ 488 2319 🕐 Mon–Sat 6:30AM–8:30PM 🚍 57, 64, 65, 70, 75, 81, 170 to Via Nazionale

BABINGTON'S TEA ROOMS

Only the well-heeled and tourists visit Babington's, established by a pair of English spinsters in 1896. Prices are astronomical, but the tea is the best in Rome (not the cakes).
🚼 fl, D5 ⊠ Piazza di Spagna 23 ☎ 678 6027 🕐 Wed–Mon 9AM–8PM 🚇 Spagna 🚍 119 to Piazza di Spagna

BERNASCONI

Famous and central. All Rome seems to congregate here on Sunday after church to drink coffee and buy cakes for Sunday lunch.
🚼 elll, D6 ⊠ Largo di Torre Argentina 15 ☎ 683 08141 🕐 Mon–Sat 6AM–1PM 🚍 44, 46, 56, 60, 61, 64, 65, 70, 75, 81, 87, 90, 170, 492, 710 to Largo di Torre Argentina

CAFFÈ GRECO

Rome's most famous and historic (but no longer its best) coffee shop, founded in 1767. Plush and atmospheric.
🚼 fl, D4 ⊠ Via Condotti 86 ☎ 678 2554 🕐 Mon–Sat 8AM–9PM 🚇 Spagna 🚍 119 to Piazza di Spagna or 52, 53, 58, 61, 71, 85, 160 to Piazza San Silvestro

CAMILLONI

A long-time rival to Sant'Eustachio, with whom it shares a piazza.
🚼 ell, D5 ⊠ Piazza Sant'Eustachio 54 ☎ 271 6068 🕐 Tue–Sun 8AM–9PM 🚍 119 to Piazza della Rotonda or 70, 81, 87, 90, 186, 492 to Corso del Rinascimento

DAGNINO

Not even the customers have changed in this superb 1950s *pasticceria* famous for Sicilian specialties, lemon water ices, and fine ice cream.
🚼 hl, E5 ⊠ Galleria Esedra, Via V. E. Orlando 75 ☎ 481 8660 🕐 Mon–Fri, Sun 7:30AM–10:30PM 🚇 Spagna 🚍 57, 64, 65, 75, 170, 492, 910 to Piazza della Repubblica

KRECHEL

Fine, expensive cakes and chocolates in an up-scale shopping street.
🚼 fl, D5 ⊠ Via Frattina 134 ☎ 678 0946 🕐 Mon–Sat 8:30AM–8:30PM 🚇 Spagna 🚍 119 to Piazza di Spagna

LA TAZZA D'ORO

The "Cup of Gold" sells only coffee, and probably the city's best espresso.
🚼 ell, D5 ⊠ Via degli Orfani 84 ☎ 678 9792 🕐 Mon–Sat 7AM–8PM 🚍 119 to Piazza della Rotonda or 70, 81, 87, 90, 186, 492 to Corso del Rinascimento

SANT'EUSTACHIO

A rival of Tazza d'Oro for the best cup of coffee, and with a welcoming interior; tables outside.
🚼 ell, D5 ⊠ Piazza Sant' Eustachio 82 ☎ 686 1309 🕐 Tue–Sun 8:30AM–1AM 🚍 119 to Piazza della Rotonda or 70, 81, 87, 90, 186, 492 to Corso del Rinascimento

Breakfast and coffee

Breakfast in Rome consists of a sweet and sometimes cream-filled croissant (*un cornetto* or *brioche*) washed down with a cappuccino or the longer and milkier *caffè latte*. At other times espresso, a short kick-start of caffeine, is the coffee of choice (Italians never drink cappuccino after lunch or dinner).

Decaffeinated coffee is *caffè Hag*, iced coffee *caffè freddo*, and American-style coffee (long and watery) *caffè Americano*. Other varieties include *caffè corretto* (with a dash of grappa or brandy) and *caffè macchiato* (espresso "stained" with a dash of milk).

69

SHOE SHOPS

Shopping areas

Although Rome's individual neighborhoods boast their own butchers, bakers, and corner shops (alimentari), most of the city's quality and speciality shops are concentrated in specific areas. Via Condotti and its surrounding grid of streets (Via Frattina, Via Borgognana, and Via Bocca di Leone) contain most of the big names in men's and women's fashion, accessories, jewelry and luxury goods. In nearby Via del Babuino and Via Margutta the emphasis is on top-price antiques, paintings, sculpture, and modern glassware and lighting. Via della Croce, which runs south from Piazza di Spagna, is known for its food shops, while Via del Corso, which bisects the northern half of central Rome, is home to inexpensive mid-range clothes, shoes, and accessories stores. Similarly, cheap stores can also be found along Via del Tritone and Via Nazionale. Nice areas to wander browsing for antiques, even if you are not buying, include Via Giulia, Via dei Coronari, Via dell'Orso, Via dei Soldati, and Via del Governo Vecchio.

BATA

A well-known and well-respected chain devoted predominantly to casual footwear. It also sells children's shoes.

gl, D5 Via dei Due Macelli 45 679 1570 Tue–Sat 9:30–7:30; Mon 3:30–7:30

BELTRAMI

One of Rome's most impressive looking shops, Beltrami is a name fabled for its superlative shoes and leather bags.

fl, D5 Via Condotti 18–19 679 1330 Mon–Sat 10–7:30

BRUNO MAGLI

A middle to up-scale chain with a choice of classic styles.

fl, D5 Via Barberini 94 and Via Vittorio Veneto 70a and Via Cola di Rienzo 237 486 850 488 4355 324 1759 Tue–Sat 9:30–7:30; Mon 1–7:30

CAMPANILE

In chic Via Condotti, this is dedicated to the most elegant (and expensive) shoes and styles.

fl, D5 Via Condotti 58 678 3041 Tue–Sat 9:30–7:30; Mon 3:30–7:30

FAUSTO SANTINI

An iconoclastic designer whose witty, innovative and occasionally bizarre shoes are aimed at the young and daring.

fl, D5 Via Frattina 122 678 4114 Tue–Sat 10–7:30; Mon 3:30–7:30

FERRAGAMO

Probably Italy's best-known shoe store, though branches grace exclusive shopping streets the world over.

fl, D5 Via Condotti 73–4 and Via Condotti 66 679 1565 678 1130 Tue–Sat 10–7; Mon 3–7:30

FRATELLI ROSSETTI

This family company, founded 30 years ago by the brothers Renzo and Renato, pushes Ferragamo (another long-established family firm) hard for the title of Italy's best shoe store. Classic and current styles at slightly lower prices than its rival.

fl, D5 Via Borgognona 5a 678 2676 Tue–Sat 9:30–7:30; Mon 3:30–7:30

MARIO VALENTINO

Exquisitely made shoes from another Rome-based Neapolitan designer. Also designs and sells leather clothing, bags and accessories.

fl, D5 Via Frattina 84 679 1246 Tue–Sat 9:30–7:30; Mon 3–7:30

POLLINI

Up-to-the-minute boots and bags for men and women in lively styles.

fl, D5 Via Frattina 22–4 678 9028 Tue–Sat 10–1, 3–7:30; Mon 3–7:30

RAPHAEL SALATO

None of Rome's cobblers come cheap, and Salato's sublimely crafted shoes are no exception. More individual than the likes of Ferragamo.

gl, E5 and fl, D5 Via Veneto 149 and Piazza di Spagna 34 482 1816 679 5646 Tue–Sat 9:30–7:30; Mon 3:30–7:30

LEATHER GOODS & ACCESSORIES

BELTRAMI
Finest quality shoes and leather goods, particularly bags, are the mainstay of this famous and decadently decorated shop in the heart of Rome's premier shopping district.

🔲 fl, D5 ✉ Via Condotti 18–19 ☎ 679 1330 🕐 Mon–Sat 10–7:30

BORSALINO
This shop is on one of the city's less exclusive shopping streets, but is still the first port-of-call if you are looking to buy a hat in Rome.

🔲 glll, D6 ✉ Via IV Novembre 157b ☎ 679 4192 🕐 Mon–Sat 9–8

CALZA E CALZE
A cornucopia of socks, stockings, and tights in every color and style imaginable.

🔲 fl, D5 ✉ Via della Croce 78 ☎ No phone 🕐 Tue–Sat 9:30–1, 3:30–7:30; Mon 3:30–7:30

FENDI
A famous family-run high-fashion name whose burgeoning Via Borgognana shop deals in both clothes and fine leather goods.

🔲 fl, D5 ✉ Via Borgognona 36a–39 ☎ 679 7641 🕐 Mon–Sat 10–2, 3–7:30

GUCCI
Recovering from the turmoils of the 1980s, when tax problems and family feuds threatened to destroy the business, this famous family name is once more in the ascendant. Expensive and high-quality bags, shoes and leather goods are a feature of this elegant shop on the Via Condoti.

🔲 fl, D5 ✉ Via Condotti 8 ☎ 678 9340 🕐 Tue–Sat 10–2, 3–7; Mon 3–7

MEROLA
Specializes in a wide range of highly-priced gloves and scarves.

🔲 fl, D5 ✉ Via del Corso 143 ☎ 679 1961 🕐 Tue–Sat 9.30–7.30; Mon 3.30–7.30

SERGIO DI CORI
Romans in search of gloves know they need look no further than this shop, which is devoted to almost nothing else.

🔲 fl, D5 ✉ Piazza di Spagna 53 ☎ 678 4439 🕐 Tue–Sat 9:30–7:30; Mon 1–7:30

SERMONETA
Also specializes in gloves, though is not as famous as its nearby rival, Sergio di Cori.

🔲 fl, D5 ✉ Piazza di Spagna 61 ☎ 679 1960 🕐 Tue–Sat 9:30–7:30; Mon 3:30–7:30

SIRNI
Exquisite artisan-made bags and briefcases crafted on the premises are the great attraction of this shop.

🔲 D5 ✉ Via della Stelletta 33 ☎ 6880 5248 🕐 Tue–Sat 9:30–1:30, 3:30–7:30; Mon 3:30–7:30

VALEXTRA
This shop close to Piazza di Spagna sells a wide range of traditional bags, briefcases, and other leather goods.

🔲 D4 ✉ Via del Babuino 94 ☎ 679 2323 🕐 Mon–Sat 10–7

Jewelry

Jewelry, and lots of it, is a key part of any Roman woman's wardrobe. Gold, in particular, is popular, and is still worked in small artisan's studios in the Jewish Ghetto, around Via Giulia and Campo de'Fiori and on Via dei Coronari, Via dell'Orso, and Via del Pellegrino. For striking costume jewelry try Delettré (Via Fontanella Borghese) or Bozart (Via Bocca di Leone 4). For a more traditional look visit Massoni (Largo Carlo Goldoni 48), founded in 1790, or Petocchi (Piazza di Spagna), jewelers to Italy's former royal family from 1861 to 1946. For the purchase of a lifetime, visit the most famous of Italian jewelers, Bulgari, whose shop at Via Condotti 10 is one of the most splendid in the city.

Food & Wine Shops

Local shopping

Roman supermarkets are few and far between (see panel opposite) and most shopping for food is still done in tiny neighborhood shops known as *alimentari*. Every street of every "village" or district in the city has one or more of these general stores, a source of everything from olive oil and pasta to candles and corn treatments. They are also good places to buy picnic provisions—many sell bread and wine—and most have a delicatessen counter that will make you a sandwich (*panino*) from the meats and cheese on display. For something a little more up-scale, or for food gifts to take home, visit the shops on Via della Croce, a street that is particularly known for its wonderful delicatessens.

AI MONASTERI

This unusual, large and rather dark old shop sells the products of seven Italian monasteries, from honeys, wines, natural preserves, and liqueurs to herbal cures and elixirs.
🚹 ell, C5 ✉ Piazza Cinque Lune 76 ☎ 6880 2783 🕐 Mon–Wed, Fri, Sat 9–1, 4:40–7:30. Closed first week of Sep

CASTRONI

Castroni boasts Rome's largest selection of imported delicacies, a mouth-watering array of Italian specialties and an outstanding range of coffees.
🚹 C4 ✉ Via Cola di Rienzo 196 ☎ 687 4383 🕐 Mon–Sat 8–8

CATENA

Founded in 1928 this luxury food store sells Italian hams, cheeses, coffees, regional delicacies, and vintage wines and liqueurs.
🚹 F7 ✉ Via Appia Nuova 9 ☎ 7049 1664 🕐 Tue–Sat 9:30–1, 3:30–7:30; Mon 3:30–7:30

ENOTECA AL GOCCETTO

Wines from all Italy are sold in this old bishop's palazzo, complete with original floors and a lovely wooden ceiling.
🚹 dll, C5 ✉ Via dei Banchi Vecchi 14 ☎ 686 4268 🕐 Mon–Sat 10:30–1:30, 5–9

ENOTECA BUCCONE

Rome's most select and best-stocked wine shop occupies a 17th-century coach house.
🚹 D4 ✉ Via di Ripetta 19–20 ☎ 361 2154 🕐 Mon–Sat 9–1:30, 4–8:30. Closed Aug

PIETRO FRANCHI

A rival to nearby Castroni for the title of Rome's "best delicatessen," offering a selection of regional food and wines, and dishes to take out—anything from cold *antipasti* to succulent roast meats.
🚹 C4 ✉ Via Cola di Rienzo 204 ☎ 683 2669 🕐 Mon–Sat 8AM–9PM

ROFFI ISABELLI

A beautiful old-fashioned shop where you can buy wine by the bottle or sip by the glass amid trickling fountains and marble-topped tables.
🚹 fl, D5 ✉ Via della Croce 76b ☎ 679 0896 🕐 Mon–Sat 10AM–11:30PM

SALUMERIA FOCACCI

One of the best delicatessens in a street renowned for its food shops. Other excellent outlets in the vicinity include Fratelli Fabbi, ✉ Via della Croce 27, a good all-round *alimentari*; and Fior Fiore, ✉ Via della Croce 17–18, known for its pizzas, pastas, and pastries.
🚹 fl, D5 ✉ Via della Croce 43 ☎ 679 1228 🕐 Mon–Wed, Fri, Sat 8:30–1:30, 4:30–7:30; Thu 8:30–1:30

VINCENZO TASCIONI

This most famous of Roman neighborhood shops sells fresh pasta, in total offering over 30 different varieties, all made on the premises.
🚹 C4 ✉ Via Cola di Rienzo 211 ☎ 324 3152 🕐 Mon–Wed, Fri, Sat 8–1:30, 4:30–7:30; Thur 4:30–7:30

STREET MARKETS

CAMPO DE' FIORI

This picturesque, central market is in a pretty square. Fruit and vegetables dominate, but you can also buy fish, flowers and beans or just watch the streetlife.

🚩 elll, c6 ✉ Piazza Campo de' Fiori 🕐 Mon–Sat 7AM–1:30PM

MERCATO ANDREA DORIA

A large, local market serving the neighborhood residents northwest of the Vatican. Stalls sell meat, fish, fruit, and vegetables, but there are a few with shoes and quality clothes.

🚩 B4 ✉ Via Andrea Doria–Via Tunisi 🕐 Mon–Sat 7AM–1PM

MERCATO DEI FIORI

Not to be confused with Campo de' Fiori, this wholesale flower market in a covered hall is opened to the public only on Tuesdays. Prices are extremely reasonable for all manner of cut flowers, potted plants and exotic Mediterranean blooms.

🚩 B4 ✉ Via Trionfale 🕐 Tue 7AM–1PM

MERCATO DELLE STAMPE

Tucked away, about a dozen stalls sell old books, magazines, and prints. Be sure to haggle.

🚩 el, D5 ✉ Largo della Fontanella di Borghese 🕐 Mon–Sat 7AM–1PM

MERCATO DI PIAZZA VITTORIO

Stallholders in central Rome's biggest and most colorful general market are fighting plans to restore the square to its 19th-century grandeur and move the stalls to nearby Via Giolitti.

🚩 F6 ✉ Piazza Vittorio Emanuele II II 🕐 Mon–Sat 7AM–2PM

MERCATO DI VIA SANNIO

This market in the shadow of San Giovanni in Laterano sells bags, belts, shoes, toys, and cheap clothes. Stalls nearby peddle more interesting bric-a-brac and secondhand clothes.

🚩 F7 ✉ Via Sannio 🕐 Mon–Sat 8AM–1PM

PIAZZA COPPELLE

A tiny, attractive neighborhood food market close to the Pantheon, an oasis among the cars and tourists.

🚩 ell, D5 ✉ Piazza Coppelle 🕐 Mon–Sat 7AM–1PM

PIAZZA SAN COSIMATO

Few visitors find this mid-sized general neighborhood food market in Trastevere.

🚩 C7 ✉ Piazza San Cosimato 🕐 Mon–Sat 7AM–1PM

PORTA PORTESE

Everything and anything is for sale in this famous flea market, though prices for the few genuine antiques are high. By mid-morning the crowds are huge, so come early and guard your belongings.

🚩 C7 ✉ Via Porta Portese–Via Ippolito Nuevo 🕐 Sun 6:30AM–2PM

Supermarkets

At the other extreme to Rome's sprawling markets are its handful of supermarkets and department stores, both types of shop that are still rather alien to most Italians. The best department store is La Rinascente, which has a central branch at Via del Corso 189, and another in Piazza Fiume. Coin is also good, though a little less stylish, and is located close to San Giovanni in Laterano at Piazzale Appio 7. The larger Standa and Upim chains are more down-scale, and offer reasonably priced clothes and general household goods: Upim has branches at Via del Tritone 172, Via Nazionale 211 and Piazza Santa Maria Maggiore; Standa's Rome branches are at Viale Trastevere 60, Via Appia Nuova 181–183, and Via Cola di Rienzo 173.

BOOKSTORES & STATIONERS

Foreign newspapers

If you need to keep in touch with what is happening at home foreign newspapers can be bought at many newsstands, or *edicole*, around the city. European editions of the *International Herald Tribune*, *Financial Times*, and *The Guardian* usually hit the stands first thing in the morning with the Italian papers. Other foreign editions arrive at around 2:30PM on the day of issue, except for Sunday editions, which are usually only available from Monday morning. The best-stocked stands, which also include a wide range of foreign magazines and periodicals, are found in Piazza Colonna on Via del Corso, at Termini train station, and at the southern end of the Via Vittorio Veneto.

ECONOMY BOOK AND VIDEO CENTER
A long-established fixture of expat life, this is the largest English-language bookstore in Italy. New and second-hand titles are available. Prices are high.
🗺 hII, E5 ✉ Via Torino 136 ☎ 474 6877 🕐 Mon–Fri 9:30–7:30; Sat 9:30–1:30

FELTRINELLI
An Italy-wide chain, with well-designed shops and shelves displaying a broad range of Italian titles, and usually a reasonable choice of French-, German-, and English-language books.
🗺 eIII, C6 and 🗺 D4 and 🗺 hI, E5 ✉ Largo di Torre Argentina 5a and ✉ Via del Babuino 39–40 and ✉ Via Vittorio Emanuele II Orlando 84–6 ☎ 6880 3248 ☎ 679 7058 ☎ 484 430 🕐 Mon–Sat 9–8; Sun 10–1:30, 4–7:30

IL SIGILLO
Close by the Pantheon, this little shop specializes in fine pens, hand-printed stationery and a wide variety of objects covered in marbled paper.
🗺 eII, D5 ✉ Via della Guglia 69 ☎ 678 9667 🕐 Mon–Fri 9:30–8; Sat 9:30–1, 4:30–8

MONDADORI
This showcase shop for one of Italy's largest publishing houses sells books, maps, and music, as well as videos, posters, and greetings cards.
🗺 C4 ✉ Piazza Cola di Rienzo 81–3 ☎ 321 0323 🕐 Mon–Sat 9:30–7:30

PINEIDER
Rome's most expensive and exclusive stationers. Virtually any design can be printed onto personalized visiting or business cards.
🗺 gI, D5 and fI, D5 ✉ Via dei Due Macelli 68 and ✉ Via della Fontanella Borghese 22 ☎ 678 9013 ☎ 687 8369 🕐 Tue–Sat 10–1:30, 3–7:30; Mon 3–7:30

POGGI
Vivid pigments, exquisite papers, and the softest brushes have been on sale at Poggi's since 1825.
🗺 fIII, D6 & fII, D5 ✉ Via del Gesù 74–5 & ✉ Via Piè di Marmo 40–1 ☎ 679 5884 ☎ 6830 8014 🕐 Mon–Fri 9–1, 4–7:30; Sat 9–1

RIZZOLI
Italy's largest bookstore now appears a little dated alongside some of its newer rivals, but you should be able to find virtually any book in Italian in print (and a selection in English).
🗺 fII, D5 ✉ Galleria Colonna, Largo Chigi 15 ☎ 679 6641 🕐 Mon–Sat 9–7:30; Sun 10–1:30, 4–8

VERTECCHI
The best source of stationery, napkins, wrapping paper, and all manner of boxes, obelisks, and books covered in beautiful Florentine marbled paper.
🗺 fI, D5 and C4 ✉ Via della Croce 70 and ✉ Via dei Gracchi 179 ☎ 678 3110 ☎ 321 3559 🕐 Tue–Sat 9–7:30; Mon 3:30–7:30

CHINA, GLASS, & FABRIC SHOPS

BISES
A breathtaking range of fabrics is housed in Via del Gesù in an elegant 17th-century palazzo. At No. 63 you can find silks and other high-fashion fabrics (wools and velvets), while at No. 91 materials more suited to home furnishing are on parade.
🏢 flll, D6 🖃 Via del Gesù 63 and 🖃 Via del Gesù 91 ☎ 678 9156 ☎ 678 0941 🕐 Tue–Sat 9:30–1, 3:30–7:30; Mon 3:30–7:30

CESARI
Cesari sells linen and lingerie at Via Barberini 1 (☎ 488 1382), but is better known for its fabrics, especially furnishing materials. The shop's setting is almost as beautiful as its products.
🏢 D4 🖃 Via del Babuino 16 ☎ 361 1441 🕐 Tue–Sat 9:30–1, 3:30–7:30; Mon 3:30–7:30

CROFF CENTRO CASA
Almost a design supermarket, Croff shows many examples of furniture, linen, and household and kitchen equipment.
🏢 el, D5 🖃 Via Tomacelli 137 ☎ 687 8385 🕐 Tue–Sat 9:30–1:30, 3:30–7:30; Mon 3:30–7:30

GINORI
One of the top Italian names in modern and traditional glass and chinaware.
🏢 C4 and gl, D5 🖃 Via Cola di Rienzo 223 and 🖃 Via del Tritone 177 ☎ 324 3132 ☎ 679 3836 🕐 Tue–Sat 9:30–1:30, 3:30–7:30; Mon 3:30–7:30

MAGAZZINI FORMA E MEMORIA
A high-tech showcase for the Forma e Memoria design team spread over four floors of a converted printing works, with fine views from the top and a small bar and restaurant in the basement.
🏢 cll, B5 and C4 🖃 Vicolo Sant'Onofrio 24 and 🖃 Passeggiata di Ripetta 19 ☎ 683 2915 ☎ 6830 7622 🕐 Tue–Sat 9:30–1:30, 3:30–7:30; Mon 3:30–7:30

MYRICAE
Bold, bright, and slightly unconventional ceramics (including regional specialties), glassware and folk art are the hallmarks of this popular, reasonably priced shop.
🏢 fl, D5 🖃 Via Frattina 36 ☎ 679 5335 🕐 Tue–Sat 9:30–1, 3:30–7:30; Mon 3:30–7:30

SPAZIO SETTE
The goods spread over three floors of the splendid Palazzo Lazzaroni comprise superbly designed objects ranging from candles to clocks and corkscrews.
🏢 elll, C6 🖃 Via dei Barbieri 7 ☎ 6880 4261 🕐 Tue–Sat 9:30–1, 3:30–7:30; Mon 3:30–7:30

STILVETRO
Italian glass and china, much of it from Tuscany, make this long-established shop a source for authentic and inexpensive gifts.
🏢 fl, D5 🖃 Via Frattina 56 ☎ 679 0258 🕐 Tue–Sat 9:30–2, 2:30–7:30; Mon 3:30–7:30

Gifts with a twist
For a souvenir with a difference visit the extraordinary shops on Via dei Cestari, just south of the Pantheon, which specialize in all sorts of religious clothes, candles, and vestments. Other religious souvenirs can be found in shops on Via di Porta Angelica near the Vatican. Alternatively visit the Farmacia Santa Maria della Scala (Piazza Santa Maria della Scala), an 18th-century monastic pharmacy that sells herbal remedies. For interesting toys try Città del Sole (Via della Scrofa 65). For the best in old prints and engravings (at a price) investigate the 100-year-old Casali (Piazza della Rotonda 81a) or the renowned Nardecchia (Piazza Navona 25).

75

WOMEN'S FASHION SHOPS

Sales and bargaining

Sales (*saldi*) in Rome are not always the bargains they can be in other major cities. This said, many shoe stores and top designers cut their prices drastically during the summer and winter sales (mid-July to mid-September and January to mid-March). Other lures to get you into a shop, notably the offer of *sconti* (discounts) and *vendite promozionali* (promotional offers), rarely save you any money in practice. While bargaining has all but died out, it can still occasionally be worth asking for a discount (*uno sconto*), particularly if you are paying cash (as opposed to using a credit card) for an expensvie item, or if you are buying several items from one shop.

FENDI
From recent beginnings (in high-fashion furs), the Fendi sisters have built a powerful fashion, perfume and accessories empire. Clothes are classic, sleek, and stylish.
✚ fl, D5 ✉ Via Borgognona 36a–39 ☎ 679 7641 🕐 Mon–Sat 10–2, 3–7:30

GIANFRANCO FERRÈ
One of Italy's top designers. His Rome outlet is known for its outlandish steel and black mosaic décor.
✚ fl, D5 ✉ Via Borgognona 42c ☎ 679 0050 🕐 Tue–Sat 9:30–1:30, 3:30–7:30; Mon 3:30–7:30

GIANNI VERSACE
Flashier and trashier than Ferrè or Armani, Versace's bright, bold color combinations need panache (and cash) to carry them off. His cheaper diffusion range, Versus, has an outlet at Via Borgognona 33–4.
✚ fl, D5 ✉ Via Bocca di Leone 26 ☎ 678 0521 🕐 Tue–Sat 10–7:30; Mon 3:30–7:30

GIORGIO ARMANI
King of cut and classic, understated elegance. His slightly cheaper range is at Via del Babuino 140 (► 77).
✚ fl, D5 ✉ Via Condotti 77 ☎ 699 1460 🕐 Mon–Sat 10–7

KRIZIA
Flies less high in the international PR and fashion firmament than the likes of Armani and Versace, but boasts a high profile in Italy, especially for knitwear.
✚ fl, D5 ✉ Piazza di Spagna 77b ☎ 679 3419 🕐 Tue–Sat 10–7; Mon 3:30–7

LAURA BIAGIOTTI
Easy to wear, easy on the eye and less aggressively "high fashion" than the other outlets in Via Borgognona.
✚ fl, D5 ✉ Via Borgognona 43–44 ☎ 679 1205 🕐 Tue–Sat 10–1:30, 3:30–7:30; Mon 10–1:30

MAX MARA
A popular mid-range label known for reliable suits, separates, knitwear, and bags and other accessories at fair prices.
✚ fl, D5 and fl, D5 ✉ Via Condotti 46 and ✉ Via Frattina 28 ☎ 678 7946 ☎ 679 3638 🕐 Tue–Sat 10–2, 3:30–7:30; Mon 3:30–7:30

TRUSSARDI
Flagship store for another of the top names in Italian fashion.
✚ fl, D5 ✉ Via Condotti 49 ☎ 679 2151 🕐 Tue–Sat 10–7:30; Mon 3:30–7:30

VALENTINO
This famous Rome designer has been dressing celebrities and the rich since the *dolce vita* days of 1959. For more affordable ready-to-wear creations visit Via Gregoriana and Via Bocca di Leone. The still cheaper "Oliver" diffusion range is on sale at Via del Babuino 61.
✚ all fl, D5 ✉ Piazza Mignanelli 22 and ✉ Via Bocca di Leone 15 and ✉ Via Gregoriana 24 ☎ 67 391 ☎ 679 5862 ☎ 67 391 🕐 Tue–Sat 10–2, 3:30–7:30; Mon 10–2

MEN'S TAILORS & CLOTHES SHOPS

BABILONIA
Famed for its garish and —by Rome standards— daring window displays, Babilonia is a favorite among young Italians looking for street-fashion essentials.
🔢 fl, D5 ✉ Via del Corso 185 ☎ 678 6641 🕐 Mon–Sat 9–8

BATTISTONI
This famous and traditional top tailoring shop has been making made-to-measure and ready-to-wear suits and shirts for over half a century.
🔢 fl, D5 ✉ Via Condotti 57 and 61a ☎ 678 6241 🕐 Tue–Sat 9:30–1:30, 3:30–7:30; Mon 3:30–7:30

CUCCI
Those members of the Roman gentry who do not patronize Battistoni probably patronize Cucci, another old-world tailor fashioning ready-to-wear and made-to-measure clothes.
🔢 fl, D5 ✉ Via Condotti 67 ☎ 679 1882 🕐 Tue–Sat 9:30–1:30, 3:30–7:30; Mon 3:30–7:30

DAVIDE CENCI
The English (or Scottish) "country gentleman's" look—tweeds, brogues, and muted classics—is hugely popular among older Italian men. This shop, established in 1926, caters to the taste, presenting its own versions of the look and originals like Burberry and Aquascutum.
🔢 ell, D5 ✉ Via Campo Marzio 1–7 ☎ 699 0681 🕐 Tue–Sat 9–1, 3:30–7:30; Mon 3:30–7:30

EMPORIO ARMANI
The "cheaper" way to buy Armani.
🔢 D4 ✉ Via del Babuino 140 ☎ 678 8454 🕐 Mon–Sat 10–7

ENZO CECI
Ready-to-wear clothes with a high-fashion bias.
🔢 fl, D5 ✉ Via della Vite 52 ☎ 679 8882 🕐 Tue–Sat 9:30–1:30, 3:30–7:30; Mon 3:30–7:30

POLIDORI UOMO
Beautifully tailored and restrained tweeds and worsted in the manner of Davide Cenci (see above): ready-to-wear or made-to-measure.
🔢 fl, D5 ✉ Via Borgognona 4a ☎ 6994 1171 🕐 Tue–Sat 9:30–1:30, 3:30–7:30; Mon 3:30–7:30

TESTA
Exquisite suits cut to appeal to a younger set.
🔢 fl, D5 and fl, D5 ✉ Via Borgognona 13 and ✉ Via Frattina 104 ☎ 679 6174 ☎ 679 1296 🕐 Tue–Sat 9:30–1:30, 3:30–7:30; Mon 3:30–7:30

VALENTINO UOMO
Sober and conservative clothes in the finest materials from Rome's leading tailor.
🔢 fl, D5 and D5 ✉ Via Condotti 13 and Oliver, Via del Babuino 61 ☎ 678 3656 ☎ 679 8314 🕐 Tue–Sat 10–2, 3:30–7:30; Mon 10–2

VERSACE UOMO
Bold, sexy clothes for lounge lizards and real or aspirant rock and film stars.
🔢 fl, D5 ✉ Via Borgognona 29 ☎ 679 5292 🕐 Tue–Sat 10–7:30; Mon 3:30–7:30

Top people's tailor

While the young turn to the mainstream Milanese designers like Armani, Rome's older and more traditional élite still choose Battistoni for their sartorial needs. Giorgio Battistoni started out almost half a century ago as a shirtmaker, but quickly graduated to the role of top-class tailor, dressing the city's older aristocracy and the more conservative hedonists of the late 1950s *dolce vita*. Clothes with the Battistoni label are still as prestigious as they were in the past, and just as costly—a custom-made shirt starts at around L300,000.

BARS BY NIGHT

What to drink

The cheapest way to drink beer in Italy is from the keg (*alla spina*). Measures are *piccola*, *media*, and *grande* (usually 33cl, 50cl, and a liter respectively). Foreign canned or bottled beers (*in lattina* or *in bottiglia*) are expensive. Italian brands like Peroni are a little cheaper: a Peroncino (25cl bottle) is a good thirst-quencher. Aperitifs (*aperitivi*) include popular non-alcoholic drinks like Aperol, Crodino, and San Pellegrino bitter. A glass of red or white wine is *un bicchiere di vino rosso/bianco*.

BAR DELLA PACE
(► 68)

TRASTÈ (► 68)

BEVITORIA
Friendlier and more intimate than most large or touristy bars on Piazza Navona. Primarily a wine bar (the cellar is part of Domitian's former stadium). Becomes busy, so arrive early.
🞤 ell, C5 ⊠ Piazza Navona 72 ☎ 6880 1022 🕒 Mon–Sat 2PM–1AM 🚍 46, 62, 64 to Corso Vittorio Emanuele II or 70, 81, 87, 90 to Corso del Rinascimento

CAVOUR 313
At the Forum end of Via Cavour, this easily missed wine bar has a relaxed, student feel. Good snacks from the bar, and wine by the glass or bottle, at tables to the rear. A good alternative to tourist bars nearby.
🞤 glll, E6 ⊠ Via Cavour 313 ☎ 678 5496 🕒 Mon–Sat 10–3:30, 7:30–11:30 🚍 11, 27, 81 to Via Cavour or 85, 87, 186 to Via dei Fori Imperiali

DRUID'S DEN
Friendly and authentic Irish pub that appeals to Romans and expats alike. Also try The Fiddler's Elbow, a popular sister pub around the corner at Via dell'Olmata 43.
🞤 E6 ⊠ Via San Martino ai Monti 28 ☎ 4890 4781 🕒 Tue–Sun 8PM–1PM 🚇 Cavour 🚍 11 to Via G. Lanzi or 27, 81 to Via Cavour or 4, 9, 14, 16 to Piazza Santa Maria Maggiore

HEMINGWAY
Although rather languid and decadent, this atmospheric and highly priced bar has for years been the favored watering hole of the city's gilded youth.
🞤 ell, D5 ⊠ Piazza Coppelle 10 ☎ 686 4490 🕒 Daily 9PM–12:30AM 🚍 70, 81, 87, 90 to Corso del Rinascimento

IL PICCOLO
This intimate and pretty little wine bar close to Piazza Navona is ideal for a romantic interlude.
🞤 dll, C5 ⊠ Via del Governo Vecchio 74–5 ☎ 6880 1746 🕒 Mon–Fri 11AM–2AM; Sat, Sun 7PM–2AM 🚍 46, 62, 64 to Corso Vittorio Emanuele II

LA VINERIA REGGIO
There is no better place in Rome to see the more rough-and-ready side of night-time drinking. Fusty and old-fashioned inside, with characters to match; tables on the city's most evocative square.
🞤 elll, C6 ⊠ Campo de' Fiori 15 ☎ 6880 3268 🕒 Mon–Sat 10:30–1:30, 6–11:45 🚍 46, 62, 64 to Corso Vittorio Emanuele II or 70, 81, 87, 90 to Corso del Rinascimento

TRIMANI
A wine bar recently added to the city's oldest wine shop (founded 1821 and still in the same family). Away from the key nightlife areas, but well placed if you find yourself near Stazione Termini.
🞤 E5 ⊠ Via Cernaia 37b ☎ 446 9630 🕒 Mon–Sat 11:30–3, 5:30–11:30 🚍 60, 61, 62 to Via Cernaia or services to Termini and Piazza della Repubblica

CLUBS & DISCOS

ALIEN

An *Alien*-inspired refit and up-to-the-minute music policy has turned this futuristic club into one of Rome's nightspots of the moment. 🚩 E4 ✉ Via Velletri 13 ☎ 841 2212 🕐 Tue–Sun 11PM–4AM 🚌 20N, 21N to Piazza Fiume 💶 Very expensive

BLACK OUT

Regaining the reputation it won over a decade ago as one of the best of the more alternative discos. Music is mainly punk, thrash, Gothic—"dark" in Roman parlance. 🚩 F7/F8 ✉ Via Saturnia 18 ☎ 7049 6791 🕐 Fri–Sat 10PM–4AM; Sun 4:30–7:30PM 🚇 Re di Roma 🚌 55N and 4, 87, 673 to Piazza Tuscolo 💶 Moderate

GILDA

If you like the Hemingway (see opposite page) then you will like Gilda, whose louche atmosphere has been attracting stars, VIPs and wanna-bes for years. There is a bar, two stylish restaurants, and a glittering dance floor. 🚩 f1, D5 ✉ Via Mario de' Fiori 97 ☎ 679 7396 🕐 Tue–Sun 11PM–5AM 🚇 Spagna 🚌 52, 53, 58, 61, 71, 85, 160 to Piazza San Silvestro 💶 Expensive

L'ALIBI

Primarily, but not exclusively a gay disco, L'Alibi is one of the most reliable (and also longest-established) of the clubs now mushrooming in the newly trendy Testaccio district. 🚩 D8 ✉ Via Monte Testaccio 44–57 ☎ 574 3448 🕐 Tue–Sun 11PM–2:30AM 🚇 Piramide 🚌 11, 13, 23, 27, 30, 57, 718 to Piazza di Porta San Paolo 💶 Winter free; depending on evening; summer moderate

LE STELLE

Another chic disco that has been running longer than most. Convenient to downtown, just northwest of Piazza del Popolo. Le Stelle is renowned for staying open until dawn. 🚩 C4 ✉ Via Cesare Beccaria 22 ☎ 361 1240 🕐 Tue–Thu, Sun 10:30PM–3AM; Fri, Sat 10:30PM–dawn 🚇 Flaminio 🚌 119 to Piazza del Popolo or 81, 90, 926 to Ponte Regina Margherita 💶 Very expensive

PIPER

Rome's clubs and discos fade in and out of fashion from one season to the next. Piper, which has been open since the 1960s, is among the more consistently popular, thanks partly to its program of constant updating and refurbishment. 🚩 F3 ✉ Via Tagliamento 9 ☎ 855 5398 🕐 Wed–Sat 10PM–5AM; Sun 3:30–7PM, 10PM–5AM 🚌 6N, 56, 57, 319 to Via Tagliamento 💶 Very expensive

RADIO LONDRA

Currently among the trendiest club-cum-discos in the city. Small and invariably full to bursting. 🚩 D8 ✉ Via Monte Testaccio 57 ☎ No phone 🕐 Tue–Sun 10:30PM–5AM 🚌 13, 23, 27, 57, 95, 716 to Via Marmorata 💶 Free

Membership and admission

Many Roman clubs and discos are run as private clubs (Associazioni Culturali), usually to circumvent planning or licensing laws. In practice this usually only means you have to buy a "membership card" (*una tessera*) in addition to the usual admission fee. The latter are high for the stylish places—mainly because Romans drink modestly and so clubs make little on their bar takings (admission usually includes a free first drink).

Opera & Classical Music

Church music

Following a decree from Pope John Paul II all concert programs in Roman churches currently have a marked religious bias. Music can range from small-scale organ recitals to full-blown choirs and orchestras. Be on the lookout for posters advertising concerts outside churches and around the city. The Coro della Cappella Giulia sing at 10:30AM and 5PM on Sundays in St. Peter's. You can hear Gregorian chant every Sunday at 11AM in Sant'Apollinare, while Sant'Ignazio di Loyola is one of the churches that regularly hosts choral concerts.

ACCADEMIA BAROCCA

Although one of the city's smaller musical associations, this Accademia's recitals reflect Rome's affinities with the baroque. Recitals, most of which are held in the Palazzo della Cancelleria on Piazza Farnese, or in the church of San Paolo entro le Mura in Via Nazionale, are not held on fixed days, so look out for flyers with details and dates of performances.

➕ ell1 and hl1, C5 and C6
✉️ Palazzo della Cancelleria, San Paolo entro le Mura ☎ 6641 1152

ACCADEMIA FILARMONICA ROMANA

Founded in 1821, the Accademia Filarmonica Romana numbered Rossini, Verdi and Donizetti among its distinguished early members. Though it does not support its own choir or orchestra, it presents high-quality recitals of contemporary, choral, and symphonic music by top-name national and international performers. Concerts are held on Thursdays (occasionally Tuesdays) from mid-October to mid-May at either the Sala Casella (details as below) or the nearby Teatro Olimpico (see opposite).

➕ C2 ✉️ Via Flaminia 118 ☎ 320 1752 🕐 Box Office daily 9AM–1PM, 6–7PM; Information daily 3–7PM 🚌 225, 910 to Piazza Antonio Mancini

ACCADEMIA NAZIONALE DI SANTA CECILIA

In existence since the 16th century, Rome's main classical music body stages concerts by its own orchestra and choir and organizes recitals and concerts by visiting choirs and orchestras. Most events are held at the Auditorio Pio also known as the Auditorio di Santa Cecilia (see opposite). Outdoor recitals and ballet performances are held in July in the Villa Giulia (➤ 35 ☎ 678 6428 or 678 0742/3/4/5 for information).

➕ f1, D4 ✉️ Via Vittoria 6 ☎ 678 0742

ASSOCIAZIONE GIOVANILE MUSICA (AGIMUS)

Agimus is a well-respected and predominantly choral body that also organizes piano and other recitals. Its concert season runs from mid-October to mid-June. Performances are usually held in the Sala Accademica (details below) or the Aula del Pontificio Istituto di Musica Sacra (see opposite).

➕ D5 ✉️ Sala Accademica, Via dei Greci 18 ☎ 678 9258 🚌 119 to Via del Corso-Via Condotti

AUDITORIO DEL FORO ITALICO

Rome's premier state-owned auditorium is part of the Mussolini-era sports city in the northwest. It is home to the orchestra of RAI, the

national radio and
television company.
🏛 B2 ✉ Piazza Lauro De Bossis
☎ 3686 5625 🎵 Concerts
Nov–Jun, Fri 6:30PM; Oct, Fri
6:30PM, Sat 9PM. Box Office
Thur–Sat 10–1, 4–7 🚌 32, 186,
280, 291, 391 to Lungotevere
Maresciallo Cadorna

AUDITORIO PIO (AUDITORIO DI SANTA CECILIA)

🏛 cII, B5 ✉ Via della
Conciliazione 4 ☎ 6880 1044
🎵 Concerts Oct–Jun, Thu–Tue
8:30 🚌 64 to Piazza San Pietro
or 23, 34, 41, 46, 62, 65, 98, 280,
881 to Ponte Vittorio Emanuele II

AULA DEL PONTIFICIO ISTITUTO DI MUSICA SACRA

🏛 eII, C5 ✉ Piazza
Sant'Agostino 20a ☎ 678 9258
🚌 119 to Piazza Cinque Lune or
70, 81, 87, 90, 186, 492 to Corso
della Rinascimento

AULA MAGNA DELL'UNIVERSITÀ SAPIENZA

🏛 G5 ✉ Piazzale Aldo Moro
☎ 361 0052 🎵 Concerts
Oct–May, Tue 8:30PM and Sat 5:30PM
🚌 9, 310 to Viale dell'Università

IL GONFALONE

The Gonfalone is a
small but prestigious
company that hosts
chamber music and
other small-scale recitals
at its own Oratorio.
🏛 dIII, C6 ✉ Oratorio del
Gonfalone, Via del Gonfalone 32a.
Information: Vicolo della Scimmia 1b
☎ 4770 4664 or 687 5952
🎵 Concerts Oct–Jun, Thur 9PM.
Box Office: Mon–Fri 9AM–1PM, day
of concert 9AM–9PM 🚌 46, 62, 64
to Corso Vittorio Emanuele or 23,
41, 65, 280 to Lungotevere di
Sangallo

ISTITUTO UNIVERSITARIO DEI CONCERTI (IUC)

The IUC's student bias
ensures exciting and
eclectic music. Concert
cycles are currently
devoted to the music
and composers of a
different country each
year. Most recitals are
held in the university's
Aula Magna just east of
Stazione Termini.
🏛 B2 ✉ Lungotevere Flaminio
50 ☎ 361 0051/2 🎵 Box
Office Mon–Fri 10AM–1PM, 3–6PM;
Sat 10AM–1PM 🚌 225, 910 to
Piazza Mancini

TEATRO DELL'OPERA

Rome's opera house is
enduring lean times,
crippled by
mismanagement and
dwindling finances, with
the reputation of its
orchestra and choir and
the quality and range of
performances
diminished. Austerity
has forced a
concentration on the
mainstream repertoire.
The opera season runs
from December to May;
recitals are held from
November to June and
in July operas are staged
outdoors at the Terme di
Caracalla (though they
may soon be moved
elsewhere). Tickets
from Via Firenze 72
(details below).
🏛 hII, E5 ✉ Via Firenze 72
☎ 481 601 🚇 Termini 🚌 57,
64, 65, 70, 71, 75, 170 to Via
Nazionale or services to Termini

TEATRO OLIMPICO

🏛 C2 ✉ Piazza Gentile da
Fabriano ☎ 323 4890 🚌 225,
910 to Piazza Mancini

Music outdoors

Al fresco recitals take place in:
the cloisters of Santa Maria della
Pace in July (part of the
"Serenate in Chiostro" season);
in the Villa Doria Pamphili in July
(as part of the the "Festival Villa
Pamphili"); in the grounds of
the Villa Giulia in the summer (as
part of the "Stagione Estivi
dell'Orchestra dell'Accademia di
Santa Cecilia"); and in the Area
Archeologica del Teatro di
Marcello from July to September
(as part of the "Estate al
Tempietto," also known as the
"Concerti del Tempietto").

LIVE MUSIC SPOTS

Listings and tickets

For details of upcoming events, consult the free *Trovaroma* listings supplement published with the Thursday edition of *La Repubblica*. Otherwise see the daily listings of *Il Messaggero*. Tickets for events can bought at the door, from the fashion shop Babilonia (▶ 77) or from ticket agencies like Orbis, ⊠ Piazza Esquilino 37 (☎ 482 7403) or Box Office, ⊠ Via Giulio Cesare 88 (☎ 372 0215). As with clubs and discos (▶ 79), you may need to buy an annual membership card (*una tessara*) on top of a ticket. Note that virtually all clubs close between late July and early September.

ALEXANDERPLATZ
A restaurant and cocktail bar north of St. Peter's with live jazz.
🚩 B4 ⊠ Via Ostia 9 ☎ 372 9398 🕐 Sep–Jun Mon–Sat 9PM–1:30AM 🚇 Ottaviano 🚌 29N, 30N, 99N, and 23, 70, 291, 490, 913, 991, 994, 999 to Largo Trionfale-Viale delle Milizie 🎟 Four-month membership (expensive); free to tourists on production of passport.

BIG MAMA
Rome's best blues club, though Big Mama also hosts rock and jazz gigs.
🚩 C4 ⊠ Vicolo San Francesca a Ripa 18 ☎ 581 2551 🕐 Oct–Jun daily 9PM–1:30AM 🚌 13, 44, 75, 170, 181, 280, 717 to Viale di Trastevere 🎟 One-year membership (very expensive) plus entry fee for some concerts

CAFFÈ LATINO
Longest established of the Testaccio clubs, devoted to eating, drinking and live music. Mostly jazz, though rap, blues and other genres are represented; discos follow bands.
🚩 D8 ⊠ Via Monte Testaccio 96 ☎ 574 4020 🕐 Sep–Jul, Tue–Thu, Sun 10:30PM– 2:30AM; Fri, Sat 10:30PM–4:30AM 🚇 Piramide 🚌 13, 23, 27, 57, 95 to Via Marmorata 🎟 Annual membership (expensive)

FOLKSTUDIO
This laid-back folk and blues venue opened in the 1960s. Presents top Italian and international names.
🚩 hIII, E6 ⊠ Via Frangipane 42 ☎ 487 1063 🕐 Mid-Sep–early Jun daily 9:30PM–12 🚌 N20, N21 and 11, 27, 81, 85, 87, 186 to Via dei Fori Imperiali 🚇 Colosseo

🎟 One year membership fee (moderate) plus entry (expensive)

FONCLEA
An established mixture of bar, restaurant and club (north of St. Peter's) devoted mainly to jazz.
🚩 B5/C5 ⊠ Via Crescenzio 82a ☎ 689 6302 🕐 Mon–Thur, Sun 8PM–2AM; Fri, Sat 9PM–3AM 🚇 Ottaviano 🚌 29N, 30N and 23, 34, 49, 492, 990 to Via Crescenzio 🎟 Free until 9PM, then entry (expensive)

MELVYN'S
A glorified bar in the heart of Trastevere that plays host mainly to local rock and R&B bands.
🚩 dIV, C6 ⊠ Via del Politeama 8 ☎ 580 3077 🕐 Mon, Thu–Sun 9PM–2AM ; Tue, Wed 10PM–2AM 🚌 20N, 30N and 23, 717, 774, 780 to Ponte Garibaldi-Lungotevere Sanzio 🎟 Entry by open membership (expensive)

ST. LOUIS MUSIC CITY
Popular modern jazz and fusion club in an underground dive between Via Cavour and Colosseum.
🚩 hIV, E6 ⊠ Via del Cardello 13a ☎ 474 5076 🕐 Mon–Sat 8:30PM–2AM 🚇 Colosseo or Cavour 🚌 20N, 21N and 11, 27, 81, 85, 87, 186 to Via Cavour-Via dei Fori Imperiali 🎟 Three-month membership (expensive)

YES BRAZIL
Tiny, lively, and busy Brazilian bar. Authentic drinks, Portuguese-speaking staff, and three hours of live music nightly from 10:30PM.
🚩 C5 ⊠ Via San Francesco a Ripa 103 ☎ 581 6267 🕐 Mon–Sat 6PM–2AM 🚌 13, 44, 75, 170, 181, 280, 717 to Viale di Trastevere 🎟 Free

SPORTS

ACQUA ACETOSA

Heavily oversubscribed public sports facilities also used for rugby games and swimming tournaments.

🔲 E1 🖂 Via dei Campi Sportivi 48 ☎ 36 851 🕓 Daily 9AM–7:30PM 🚇 Acqua Acetosa or Campi Sportivi 🚌 4, 230

ALDROVANDI PALACE (SWIMMING)

Public swimming pools in Rome are either some way from the center or not terribly pleasant. Your best option is to use a hotel pool; many open to nonresidents on payment of a daily tariff.

🔲 E3 🖂 Via Aldrovandi 15, Parioli (north of Zoo & Villa Borghese) ☎ 322 4288 🕓 Daily Jun–Sep, 10–6 🚌 19, 30 to Via Aldrovandi

FORO ITALICO (TENNIS, ATHLETICS)

One of the world's finest sports complexes when built in the 1930s, the Foro Italico is today perhaps best known for the Italian open tennis tournament held here each May.

🔲 B2 🖂 Lungotevere Maresciallo Diaz-Viale dei Gladiatori 31 ☎ 36851 🚌 32, 186, 280, 291, 391 to Lungotevere Maresciallo Cadorna

IPPODROMO DELLE CAPANNELLE (HORSE RACING)

Flat racing, steeple-chasing, and trotting can all be seen at Rome's main race course.

🖂 Via Appia Nuova 1255 ☎ 718 3143 🕓 Races Sep–Jun, Mon, Wed, Fri, Sun 1:30–7:30PM 🚌 650, 671 to Via Appia Nuova

PALAZZO DELLO SPORT

Part of the EUR complex built for the 1960 Olympics, this stadium is now used for a range of indoor sports, most notably basketball (games are played on Sunday at 5:30PM).

🔲 C13 🖂 Via dell'Umanesimo ☎ 592 5006 or 592 6809 🚇 EUR Palasport

PALAZZETTO DELLO SPORT

Another stadium built for the 1960 Olympic Games. Hosts spectator sports such as boxing, fencing, tennis, and wrestling.

🔲 C2 🖂 Piazza Apollodoro-Via Flaminia 🕓 Daily 7AM–8PM 🚇 Flaminio 🚌 225, 910 to Piazza Appollodoro

STADIO OLIMPICO (SOCCER)

Rome's two big soccer teams, AS Roma and Lazio, play their home games here on alternate Sundays.

🔲 B1 🖂 Viale dei Gladiatori ☎ 3685 7520. Ticket office 323 7333 ☎ Information (AS Roma) 506 0200; (Lazio) 3685 7566 🕓 Ticket office daily 9–1:30, 2:30–6 🚌 32, 186, 280, 291, 391 to Lungotevere Maresciallo Cadorna

TRE FONTANE

Part of the extensive EUR sports facilities. Hosts different indoor spectator sports on most days of the week.

🔲 C13 🖂 Via delle Tre Fontane 🕓 Tue–Sun 7:30AM–8PM; Mon 4–8PM 🚇 Magliana 🚌 671, 707, 714, 717, 764, 771, 791 to Via delle Tre Fontane

Local rivalry

Rivalry between Rome's two Serie A (first division) soccer teams is intense. Lazio, a traditional underachiever, is currently doing as well as AS Roma, once among Italy's soccer élite (its last championship, or *scudetto*, was in 1982–1983). AS Roma is known as the *i giallorossi* (after the team's red and yellow uniform), while the blue-and-white-shirted Lazio players sport the nickname *i biancocelesti*. AS Roma's symbol is the Roman wolf-cub, Lazio's an eagle (both often seen among the city's graffiti).

LUXURY HOTELS

A single room in one of Rome's most luxurious hotels costs about L300,000 or more per night.

Booking

Rome's peak season runs from Easter to October, but the city's hotels (in all categories) are almost invariably busy. Telephone, write, or fax well in advance to book a room (most receptionists speak some English, French, or German). Leave a credit card number or send an international money order for the first night's stay to be certain of the booking. Reconfirm bookings a few days before your trip. If you arrive without a reservation, get to a hotel early in the morning; by afternoon most of the vacated rooms will have been snapped up. Don't accept rooms from touts at Stazione Termini.

AMBASCIATORI PALACE
One of the more venerable and stately of the Via Veneto's large luxury hotels with a traditional feel and opulent appearance.
✚ gI, E5 ✉ Via Vittorio Veneto 70 ☎ 47 493 🚇 Barberini 🚌 52, 53, 56, 58, 95 to Via Vittorio Veneto

DEL SOLE AL PANTHEON
A hotel since 1467; chic and the location opposite the Pantheon—if you can stand the crowds—is one of Rome's best.
✚ ell, D5 ✉ Piazza della Rotonda 63 ☎ 678 0441 🚌 119 to Piazza della Rotonda, 70, 81, 87, 90 to Corso del Rinascimento

EXCELSIOR
One of the largest and grandest of Rome's luxury hotels. Everything here is on an enormous scale, from the vast silk rugs to the palatial bedrooms.
✚ gI, E5 ✉ Via Vittorio Veneto 125 ☎ 4708 🚇 Barberini 🚌 52, 53, 56, 58, 95 to Via Vittorio Veneto

HASSLER-VILLA MEDICI
Magnificently situated and famous hotel just above the Spanish Steps, long the haunt of VIPs and the jet-set.
✚ fl, D5 ✉ Piazza Trinità dei Monti 6 ☎ 678 2651 🚇 Spagna 🚌 119 to Piazza di Spagna

HOLIDAY INN CROWNE PLAZA MINERVA ROME
A new and well-designed five-star chain hotel in the shadow of the Pantheon and Santa Maria sopra Minerva.
✚ fIll, D5 ✉ Piazza della Minerva 69 ☎ 684 1888 🚌 119 to Piazza della Rotonda, 70, 81, 87, 90 to Corso del Rinascimento

INGHILTERRA
Founded in 1850, and host to such guests as Liszt and Hemingway, this clublike hotel is near the best shopping streets.
✚ fl, D5 ✉ Via Bocca di Leone 14 ☎ 672 161 🚇 Spagna 🚌 119 to Piazza di Spagna or 52, 53, 58, 61, 71, 85, 160 to Piazza San Silvestro

LE GRAND HOTEL
Not in the most salubrious location, but an immensely opulent hotel that is often rated the most luxurious in the city.
✚ hl, E5 ✉ Via Vittorio Emanuele Orlando 3 ☎ 4709 🚇 Repubblica 🚌 57, 64, 65, 75, 170, 492, 910 to Piazza della Repubblica

LORD BYRON
A small, extremely chic and refined five-star away from the center in leafy Parioli. Particularly noted for its excellent restaurant.
✚ D3 ✉ Via G de Notaris 5 ☎ 361 3041 🚇 Flaminio 🚌 52, 926 to Via Buozzi

RAPHAEL
An intimate, charming ivy-covered hotel hidden away but close to Piazza Navona. Rooms are perhaps a little small, but renovations mean furniture and fittings are immaculate. Book ahead.
✚ ell, C5 ✉ Largo Febo ☎ 683 8881 or 682 831 🚌 70, 81, 87, 90 to Corso del Rinascimento

MID-PRICE HOTELS

CAMPO DE' FIORI

Good value, close to Campo de' Fiori. Rooms are small but pretty, and there is a roof garden.

☐ elll, C6 ☒ Via del Biscione 6
☎ 687 4886 🚌 46, 62, 64 to Corso Vittorio Emanuele II

CESARI

A thoroughly reliable, friendly and no-frills hotel with a loyal clientele. Perfectly located for the area midway between the Corso and the Pantheon.

☐ flll, D5 ☒ Via di Pietra 89a
☎ 679 2386 🚌 56, 60, 62, 85, 90, 160 to Via del Corso

COLUMBUS

A converted monastery just a minute's walk away from St. Peter's. A favorite with visiting cardinals.

☐ cll, B5 ☒ Via della Conciliazione 33 ☎ 686 5435
🚌 23, 24 to Via della Conciliazione or 64 to Piazza San Pietro

DUE TORRI

Hidden in a tiny alley between Piazza Navona and the Tiber. Rooms are all adequate, but vary from the stylish to the plain.

☐ ell, C5 ☒ Vicolo del Leonetto 23–5 ☎ 687 6983 🚌 70, 81, 87, 90, 186 to Corso del Rinascimento or Lungotevere Marzio

HOTEL PORTOGHESI

Well-known if slightly fading hotel with roof terrace situated in a cobbled street just north of Sant'Agostino and Piazza Navona.

☐ ell, C5 ☒ Via dei Portoghesi 1
☎ 686 4231 🚌 70, 81, 87, 90 to Corso del Rinascimento

LA RESIDENZA

Good choice near the Via Veneto without charging top prices. Stylish public spaces, rooms spacious and comfortable. Terrace and roof garden.

☐ E4 ☒ Via Emilia 22–4
☎ 488 0789 🚇 Barberini
🚌 52, 53, 56, 58, 95 to Via Vittorio Veneto

LOCARNO

In a quietish side street close to Piazza del Popolo. Much genuine 1920s art nouveau décor.

☐ C4 ☒ Via della Penna 22
☎ 361 0841 🚇 Flaminio
🚌 90, 119, 926 to Via di Ripetta, 81 to Lungotevere in Augusta

MANFREDI

Small, family-run hotel in a cobbled street of galleries and antique shops. Pretty and quiet.

☐ D4 ☒ Via Margutta 61
☎ 320 7676 🚇 Spagna
🚌 119 to Via del Babuino

MARGUTTA

Quaint hotel near Piazza del Popolo between the Corso and Via del Babuino. Public areas a little spartan, but the redecorated rooms are bright and comfortable.

☐ D4 ☒ Via Laurina 34
☎ 679 8440 🚇 Spagna
🚌 119 to Piazza di Spagna

SISTINA

Small, reliable, and efficient hotel close to the Piazza di Spagna. Lovely terrace for drinks and summer breakfasts.

☐ gl, D5 ☒ Via Sistina 136
☎ 4890 0316 🚇 Spagna or Barberini 🚌 119 to Piazza di Spagna, 52, 53, 56, 58, 60, 61, 62 to Piazza Barberini

Expect to pay L125,000–300,000 per night for a single room in a mid-price hotel.

Prices

Italy's hotels are classified into five categories from one-star (basic) to five-star (luxury). The prices each can charge are set by law and must be displayed in the room (usually on the door). Prices within a hotel, however, can vary for different rooms (and some hotels have low- and high-season rates). Therefore if a room is too expensive, do not be afraid to inquire if there is anything cheaper. Look out for extras like air conditioning or obligatory breakfasts. Single rooms cost about two thirds the price of doubles, and to add an extra bed to a room adds 35 percent to the bill.

BUDGET ACCOMMODATIONS

Budget accommodations can cost anything up to L125,000 per night for a single room.

Noise

Noise is a fact of life in almost any Roman hotel (in whatever price category). Surveys have shown Rome to be the noisiest city in Europe. You will never escape the cacophony entirely (unless the hotel is air conditioned and double-glazed), but to lessen the potential racket you should avoid main thoroughfares and the area around Termini in favor of hotels near parks or in more obscure back streets. Also try asking for rooms away from the front of the hotel or facing on to a central courtyard (*cortile*).

ABRUZZI

Twenty-five large, basic rooms (and four shared bathrooms), some with a view of the Pantheon (noisy); rooms at the rear are quieter.

➕ ell, D5 ✉ Piazza della Rotonda 69 ☎ 679 2021 🚍 119 to Piazza della Rotonda or 44, 46, 75, 87, 94, 170 to Largo di Torre Argentina

FIORELLA

Eight bright, airy, and spotless rooms (two shared bathrooms) in a part of town with few budget-priced hotels. 1AM curfew.

➕ D4 ✉ Via del Babuino 196 ☎ 361 0597 Ⓜ Spagna 🚍 119 to Piazza di Spagna

KATTY

The Katty is less grim than most of the countless cheap hotels in the unsavory area near Rome's main train station, and its 11 rooms are always well booked.

➕ F5 ✉ Via Palestro 5 ☎ 444 1216 Ⓜ Termini 🚍 27, 64, 65, 170 and all other services to Termini

NAVONA

Simple rooms, friendly owners, and a superb central location (just west of Piazza Sant'Eustacchio) mean it is essential to book well in advance to secure one of the 26 rooms.

➕ ell, C5 ✉ Via dei Sediari 8 ☎ 686 4203 🚍 70, 81, 87, 90, 186, 492 to Corso del Rinascimento

PERUGIA

Little-known hotel, quiet and well-located, between Via Cavour and the Colosseum. All eight doubles have private bathrooms.

➕ hlV, E6 ✉ Via del Colosseo 7 ☎ 679 7200 🚍 11, 27, 81 to Via Cavour or 85, 87, 186 to the Colosseum

PICCOLO

Another fine little hotel close to Campo de' Fiori. Only half of the 16 rooms have private bathrooms.

➕ C6 ✉ Via dei Chiavari 32 ☎ 6880 2560 or 689 2330 🚍 46, 62, 64 to Corso Vittorio Emanuele II or 44, 56, 60, 65, 75, 170 to Via Arenula

POMEZIA

The 22 rooms are small (11 have private bathrooms), but the location is central and close to Campo de' Fiori. Roof terrace and small bar.

➕ elll, C6 ✉ Via dei Chiavari 12 ☎ 686 1371 🚍 46, 62, 64 to Corso Vittorio Emanuele II or 44, 56, 60, 65, 75, 170 to Via Arenula

SMERALDO

Plain, clean, and straightforward hotel located in a back street a couple of minutes' walk from the central Campo de' Fiori.

➕ elll, C6 ✉ Vicolo dei Chiodaroli 11 ☎ 687 5929 🚍 46, 62, 64 to Corso Vittorio Emanuele II or 44, 56, 60, 65, 75, 170 to Via Arenula

SOLE

A popular budget choice, on the edge of Campo de' Fiori. There are 62 rooms, but booking is essential. Small garden terrace.

➕ elll, C6 ✉ Via del Biscione 76 ☎ 6880 6873 or 6880 5258 🚍 46, 62, 64 to Corso Vittorio Emanuele II or 44, 56, 60, 65, 75, 170 to Via Arenula

ROME
travel facts

ARRIVING & DEPARTING

Before you go

- All visitors to Italy require a valid passport.
- Visas are not required for US, Canadian, UK, Irish, Australian, or New Zealand citizens, and for other EU nationals for stays of under three months.
- Vaccinations are not required unless you are coming from a known infected area.

When to go

- April to early June and mid-September to October are the best periods.
- July and August are uncomfortably hot, and many restaurants and businesses close for a month's holiday in August.
- Holy Week (Easter) is also especially busy.
- January and February are the quietest months.

Climate

- Winters are short and cold.
- Spring begins in March, but April and May can be muggy and rainy.
- Summers are hot and dry, though sudden thunderstorms are common.
- Weather in autumn is mixed, but can produce days of crisp temperatures and clear skies.

Arriving by air

- Scheduled flights arrive at Leonardo da Vinci airport, better known as Fiumicino.
- Fiumicino information: ☎6595 4455 or 6596 3640. Alitalia information: ☎65 601 or 65 621.
- Shuttle trains link Fiumicino to Stazione Termini (information: ☎4775) in the city centre.
- Taxis are slow and expensive.

Take only licensed (yellow) cabs or one of the pre-paid "car with driver" deals available from the SOCAT desk in the International Arrivals hall.

- Charter flights use Ciampino (information: ☎794 941), a military airport south of Rome.
- From Ciampino go by bus to Anagnina or Subaugusta, and then by Metro line A to Stazione Termini.

By train

- Most trains arrive and depart from Stazione Termini, well placed for most of central Rome.
- Taxis and buses leave from the station forecourt, Piazza dei Cinquecento.

Customs regulations

- EU nationals do not have to declare goods imported for their personal use.
- Limits for non-EU visitors are: 400 cigarettes or 200 small cigars or 500g of tobacco; 1 liter of spirits (over 22 percent alcohol) or 2 liters of fortified wine (over 22 percent alcohol); 50g of perfume.

ESSENTIAL FACTS

Travel insurance

- It is vital to take out full health and travel insurance before traveling to Italy.

Tourist information

- Ente Provinciale per il Turismo di Roma ✉ Via Parigi 11 ☎488 991 🕐 Mon–Sat 8:30AM–7:30PM.

Opening hours

- Stores: 🕐 Tue–Sat 8AM–1PM, 4–8PM; Mon 4–8PM (with slight seasonal variations). Food shops open on Monday mornings but

usually close on Thursday
afternoons.
- Restaurants: ⊙ 12:30–3PM,
7:30–10:30PM. Many close on
Sunday evenings and Monday
lunchtimes. Bars and restaurants
also have a statutory closing day
(*riposo settimanale*) and many close
for much of August.
- Churches: ⊙ daily 7AM–12,
4:30–7PM.
- Museums and galleries: vary
considerably; usually close on
Monday (see individual entries).
- Banks: ⊙ Mon–Fri
8:30AM–1:30PM: major branches
may also open 3–4PM.
- Post offices: ⊙ Mon–Fri
8:15AM–2PM, Sat 8:15AM–12.
The main post office in Piazza
San Silvestro opens ⊙ Mon–Fri
8AM–9PM, Sat 8AM–12 noon.

Public holidays
- Jan 1; Jan 6; Easter Monday;
Apr 25; May 1; Jun 29; Aug 15 ;
Nov 1; Dec 8; Dec 25; Dec 26 .

Money matters
- The Italian currency is the *lira*,
abbreviated to "L."
- Notes: L1,000, L2,000, L5,000,
L10,000, L50,000, and L100,000.
- Coins: L5 and L10 (both rare),
L50, L100, L200, L500, plus a
L200 telephone token (*gettone*)
which can be used as a coin.
- Most major traveler's checks can
be changed at banks, though lines
can be long.
- Credit cards (*carte di credito*) are
slowly gaining in popularity, but
cash is preferred.

Women travelers
- Women can expect some (rarely
threatening) hassle from Italian
men.
- At night avoid the parks and the
area around Termini.

Time differences
- Italy is six hours ahead of New
York and nine hours ahead of Los
Angeles.

Electricity
- Electric current is 220 volts AC,
50 cycles, with plugs of the two
"round"-pin type.

Etiquette
- Do not wear shorts, short skirts,
or skimpy tops in churches.
- Avoid entering churches while
services are in progress.
- Many churches and galleries
forbid flash photography, or
ban photography altogether.
- Smoking is common in bars and
restaurants, but banned on public
transport.
- Public drunkenness is rare and
frowned upon.

PUBLIC TRANSPORTATION

Buses and trams
- Rome's orange buses and trams,
run by ATAC, have cheap and
frequent services.
- Blue regional and suburban buses
are run by COTRAL.
- Buses are often crowded and the
city's traffic-clogged streets can
make travel slow.
- Information: ✚ F5 ⊠ ATAC
Information, Piazza dei
Cinquecento ☎ 4695 4444.
⊙ daily 7:30AM–7PM 🚇 Termini.
Tickets and information can also
be found at Piazza del
Risorgimento, Piazza San Silvestro
and at 35 green ATAC booths
dotted around the city.
- Tickets must be bought before
boarding the bus and can be
obtained from ATAC kiosks,
shops and newsstands displaying
an ATAC sticker, and at

tobacconists (indicated by signs showing a white "T" on a blue background).

- Tickets must be stamped at the at the rear of each bus or tram. They are valid for any number of rides within a 90-minute time period. Remember to enter buses by back doors, and to leave by center doors (if you have a pass or validated ticket with time to run you can also use the front doors).
- Buy several tickets at once as some outlets close early.
- There are heavy on-the-spot fines if you are caught without a ticket.
- Services: daytime services run 5:30AM–11:30PM, depending on the route. Bus stops (*fermate*) list numbers and routes of the buses they serve. Note that one-way systems mean buses often have slightly different return routes.
- Night buses: 30 night buses (*servizio notturno*) run on key routes from about midnight to 5:30AM. Unlike day buses they have a conductor who sells tickets.
- Useful services:
  23 Piazza del Risorgimento (for the Vatican Museums)–Trastevere–Piramide.
  27 Termini–Roman Forum–Colosseum–Piramide.
  46 Piazza Venezia–Vatican.
  56, **60** and **75** Piazza Venezia–Trastevere.
  64 Stazione Termini–Piazza Venezia–Corso Vittorio Emanuele II–St. Peter's.
  81 Piazza del Risorgimento (Vatican Museums)–Via Nazionale–Roman Forum–Colosseum–San Giovanni in Laterano.
  119 Circular minibus service in the historic center: Piazza Augusto Imperatore–Piazza della Rotonda (Pantheon)–Via del Corso–Piazza di Spagna.

Metro

- Rome's subway system (*la Metropolitana*, or *Metro*) has just two lines—named A and B—which intersect at Stazione Termini. Primarily a commuter service, it is of only limited use in the city center. It is good, however, for quick trans-city rides.
- Stations at Colosseo, Spagna, Barberini, Repubblica, Termini, and San Giovanni are convenient for major sights.
- Station entrances are marked by a large, red M, and each has a map of the network.
- Tickets are valid for one ride and can be bought from tobacconists (*tabacchi*), bars, and shops with ATAC or COTRAL stickers, and—if they are working—from machines at stations (exact money only). Day passes are also available.
- Services on Line A run daily 5:30AM–11:30PM and on Line B Mon–Fri 5:30AM–9:30PM, Sat and Sun 5:30AM–11:30PM.

Passes

- An integrated ticket, the *Biglietto Integrato* (BIG) is available from the sources listed above and is valid for a day's unlimited travel on ATAC buses, the Metro, COTRAL buses and the sub-urban FS rail network.
- Weekly tourist passes (*Abbonamento Settimanale per Turisti*) are valid for a week on buses and Metro only.

Taxis

- Licensed taxis: official Rome taxis are yellow (and occasionally white), with a"Taxi" sign on the roof. Use only these and refuse offers from touts at Fiumicino, Termini, and elsewhere.

- Calling a cab: the cab firm will give you a taxi code name, a number and the time it will take to get to you. The meter starts running as soon as they are called. Firms include Cosmos Radio Taxis (☎ 88 177), Autoradio Taxi (☎ 3570), and Capitale Radio (☎ 4994).

- When hailing a cab make sure the meter is set at zero. The minimum fare is valid for 3km or the first 9 minutes of a ride. Surcharges are levied between 10PM and 7AM, all day Sunday, on public holidays, for airport trips, and for each piece of luggage in the trunk.

- Drivers are not supposed to stop on the streets (though some do), and it is therefore difficult to hail a passing cab. Taxis congregate instead at stands, indicated by blue signs with *Taxi* written on them in white. Stands can be found downtown at Termini, Piazza Venezia, Largo Argentina, Piazza S. Sonnino, Pantheon, Piazza di Spagna, and Piazza San Silvestro.

MEDIA & COMMUNICATIONS

Telephones

- Public telephones are indicated by a red or yellow sign showing a telephone dial and receiver. They are found on the street, in bars and restaurants, and in special offices (*Centri Telefoni*) equipped with banks of phones and (occasionally) staff.

- A few *Centri Telefoni* have phones where you speak first and pay later, but most phones and booths require prepayment.

- Phones accept L100, L200, and L500 coins, L200 tokens known as *gettoni*, and—increasingly—

phone cards, or *schede telefoniche* (available from post offices, tobacconists, and some bars in L5,000, L10,000, and L20,000 denominations). Remember to break off the cards' small marked corner before use.

- Cheap rate for calls is Mon–Sat 10PM–8AM and all day Sunday.

Postal Service

- Stamps (*francobolli*) can be bought from post offices and most tobacconists.

- Post boxes are red and have two slots, one for Rome (marked *Per La Città*) and one for other destinations (*Per Tutte Le Altre Destinazioni*).

- The Vatican postal service is quicker (though tariffs are the same), but stamps can only be bought at the post offices in the Vatican Museums (◉ Mon–Fri 8:30AM–7PM) and in Piazza San Pietro (☎ 6982 ◉ Mon–Fri 8:30AM–7PM, Sat 8:30AM–6PM). Vatican mail can only be posted in the Vatican's blue *Poste Vaticane* mail boxes.

- Most post offices (*Posta* or *Ufficio Postale*) open Mon–Fri 8:15AM–2:30PM, Sat and the last day of each month 8:15AM to midday. The main post office, the *Ufficio Postale Centrale*, is located at Piazza San Silvestro 18–20 (☎ 6771) and opens Mon–Fri 8AM–7:30PM, Sat 8:30AM–noon.

Newspapers and magazines

- Most Romans read the Rome-based *Il Messagero*, the mainstream and authoritative *Corriere della Sera*, or the center-left and popularist *La Repubblica* (it has a special Rome edition). Sports papers and news magazines (like *Panorama* and *L'Espresso)* are also popular.

• Foreign newspapers can usually be bought after about 2:30PM on the day of issue from booths (*edicole*) in and near Termini, Piazza Colonna, Largo di Torre Argentina, Piazza Navona, Via Vittoria Veneto, and close to several other major tourist sights. European editions of the *International Herald Tribune* and *Financial Times* are also widely available.

Radio and television

• Italian television is divided between the three channels of the state network RAI, the three private channels of Silvio Berlusconi (Canale 5, Rete 4, and Italia 1), and a host of smaller commercial stations.

• RAI also runs a public radio service, although the airwaves are dominated by dozens of smaller (mainly FM) stations.

EMERGENCIES

Safety

• Carry all valuables in a belt or pouch—never in a pocket.

• Hold bags across your front, never over one shoulder, where they can be grabbed or rifled.

• Wear your camera—never put it down on a café table.

• Leave valuables and jewelry (especially chains and earrings) in the hotel safe.

• Beware the persistent small gangs of street children. If approached, hang on to everything, raise your voice and—if necessary—push them away.

• Never leave luggage or other possessions in parked cars.

• Beware pickpockets, especially in buses, crowded tourist areas and busy shopping streets (the 64 bus

to St. Peter's is notorious).

• Avoid parks and the back streets around Termini late at night.

Lost property

• To make an insurance claim on a lost or stolen piece of property report the loss to a police station, which will issue you a signed declaration (*una denuncia*) for your insurance company. The central police station is the *Questura* ☒ Via San Vitale 15 (off Via Nazionale) ☎ 4686.

• Main lost property offices are: **ATAC** (for articles lost on the bus or tram network) ☒ Via Nicola Bettoni 1 ☎ 581 6040 🕔 daily 9AM–midday Metro Line A: Furio Camillo Metro Station ☎ 5753 3620 🕔 Mon, Tue, Fri 9AM–midday **COTRAL** (suburban buses): inquire at the origin (*capolinea*) of individual routes or phone ☎ 57 531 or 591 5551 **Trains**: Stazione Termini, Via Giovanni Giolitti 24 (near Platform 22) ☎ 4730 6682 🕔 Mon–Fri 7AM–10PM

Medical and Dental Treatment

• For urgent medical treatment go to the casualty department (*Pronto Soccorso*) of the Ospedale Fatebenefratelli ☒ Isola Tiberina ☎ 58 731 or Policlinico Umberto I ☒ Viale Policlinico ☎ 446 2341.

• The American-run *George Eastman Clinic* provides a 24-hour emergency dentist service: ☒ Viale Regina Elena 287 ☎ 445 4851, 24-hour line 491 949. No credit cards.

• Pharmacies are indicated by a large green cross. Opening times are usually Mon–Sat 8:30AM–1PM, 4–8PM, but a rotating schedule (displayed on pharmacy doors) ensures at least one pharmacy is open 24 hours a day, seven days a week. The most central English-speaking pharmacist is *Internazionale* ✉ Piazza Barberini 49 ☎ 482 5456.

Key telephone numbers

- Police, Fire and Ambulance (General SOS) ☎ 113
- Ambulance (Red Cross) ☎ 5510
- Police (Carabinieri) ☎ 112
- Central Police Station ☎ 4686
- ACI Auto Assistance (Car Breakdowns) ☎ 116
- US Embassy ☎ 46741
- Samaritans ☎ 7045 4444
- Operator ☎ 12
- International Operator (Europe) ☎ 15
- International Operator (rest of the world) ☎ 170

LANGUAGE

- Italians respond well to foreigners who make an effort to speak their language (however badly). Many Italians speak some English, and most upscale hotels and restaurants have multilingual staff.
- All Italian words are pronounced as written, with each vowel and consonant sounded. The letter c is hard, as in English "cat" except when followed by i or e, when it becomes the soft ch of "children." The same applies to g when followed by i or e—soft in *giardino* (as in the English "giant"; hard in *gatto*, as in "gate"; words ending in o are almost always masculine in gender (plural— i); those ending in a are feminine (plural—e).
- Use the polite, third person (*lei*) to speak to strangers: use the second person (*tu*) to friends or children.

Courtesies

good morning	buon giorno
good afternoon/ good evening	buona sera
good night	buona notte
hello/goodbye (informal)	ciao
hello (answering the telephone)	pronto
goodbye	arrivederci
please	per favore
thank you (very much)	grazie (mille)
you're welcome	prego
how are you? (polite/informal)	come sta/stai?
I'm fine	sto bene
I'm sorry	mi dispiace
excuse me/ I beg your pardon	mi scusi
excuse me (in a crowd)	permesso

Basic vocabulary

yes/no	sí/no
I do not understand	non ho capito
left/right	sinistra/destra
entrance/exit	entrata/uscita
open/closed	aperto/chiuso
good/bad	buono/cattivo
big/small	grande/piccolo
with/without	con/senza
more/less	più/meno
near/far	vicino/lontano
hot/cold	caldo/freddo
early/late	presto/ritardo
here/there	qui/là
now/later	adesso/più tardi
today/tomorrow	oggi/domani
yesterday	ieri
how much is it?	quant'è?
when?/do you have?	quando?/avete?

Emergencies

help!	aiuto!
Where is the nearest telephone?	Dov'è il telefono più vicino?
There has been an accident.	C'è stato un incidente.
Call the police.	Chiamate la polizia.
Call a doctor/ an ambulance.	Chiamate un medico/ un'ambulanza.
first aid	pronto soccorso
Where is the nearest hospital?	Dov'è l'ospedale più vicino?

INDEX

Entries beginning San,
Santa, Santo or Santi are
indexed as if the first element
of the name were San.

ACKNOWLEDGMENTS

The Automobile Association would like to thank the following photographers, libraries and associations for their assistance in the preparation of this book.

© NIPPON TELEVISION NETWORK CORPORATION TOYKO 1991 1
SPECTRUM COLOUR LIBRARY 33b

The remaining pictures are held in the Association's own library (AA PHOTO LIBRARY) with contributions from:
M ADLEMAN 87a; J HOLMES 5a, 7, 17, 18, 19, 24a, 25, 26, 29a, 29b, 32, 33a, 37a, 38a, 39, 41b, 44, 46a, 46b, 48b, 54, 55, 57, 60; D MITIDIERI 5b, 12, 13a, 16, 23, 28, 31, 34a, 34b, 35, 38b, 43, 45a, 47, 49a, 49b, 50, 53, 58, 59a, 59b; C SAWYER 2, 6, 20, 27a, 27b, 30a, 40, 41a; A SOUTER 13b, 21; P WILSON 9, 24b, 30b, 36, 37b, 42a, 42b, 45b, 48a, 51, 52, 56, 61, 87b

Copy-editor: *Moira Johnston*
Verifier: *Kerry Fisher*
Indexer: *Marie Lorimer*
Original design: *Design FX*